LESSONS
IN
LOVE

By Anne, a lay apostle

LESSONS
IN
LOVE

By Anne, a lay apostle

ISBN: 978-1-933684-92-5

Library of Congress Number: applied for

Publisher: Direction for Our Times
9000 West 81st Street
Justice, Illinois 60458

708-496-9300
contactus@directionforourtimes.com

www.directionforourtimes.org

Direction for Our Times is a 501(c)(3) tax-exempt organization.

Manufactured in the United States of America

Graphic design and stained glass art by:
Chris Deschaine
www.braintrustdesign.com

How to Pray the Rosary information and the image of *Mary Immaculate* are used with permission. Copyright © Congregation of Marians of the Immaculate Conception, Stockbridge, MA 01263. www.marian.org

Painting of *Jesus Christ the Returning King* by Janusz Antosz
V1110

*This book is dedicated with love to 'the team',
past, present and future of Direction for Our Times.
The team includes staff and volunteers and
those who support staff and volunteers.
The team includes translators, printers, shippers and
those who hand out books, booklets and monthly
messages in many countries. May we all work for
Jesus and Mary with happy abandon.*

Direction for Our Times wishes to manifest its complete obedience and submission of mind and heart to the final and definitive judgment of the Magisterium of the Catholic Church and the local Ordinary regarding the supernatural character of the messages received by Anne, a lay apostle.

In this spirit, the messages of Anne, a lay apostle, have been submitted to her bishop, Most Reverend Leo O'Reilly, Bishop of Kilmore, Ireland, and to the Vatican Congregation for the Doctrine of the Faith for formal examination. In the meantime Bishop O'Reilly has given permission for their publication.

Table of Contents

Part One

The Place of
the Divine Will

The Narrow Door

He said to them, "Try your best to enter by the narrow door, because, I tell you, many will try to enter and will not succeed" (Luke 13:24).

One day I began to consider this Bible verse. What is this narrow door, I wondered. Why will many be unable to enter?

I think the narrow door must be the Sacred Heart of Jesus Christ, the doorway that leads each of us to the divine will in our lives. In order to truly enter into the heart of Jesus, we must serve Him in the way He needs us to serve. This is another way of saying that we must reduce our commitment to self-will and replace it with commitment to divine will. Often we pay lip service to this but do not really abandon our own plan.

Jesus says that the door is narrow. I think that means that we cannot get through it if we are carrying too much of our own *stuff.* If we are laden down, we are bulky and we simply cannot squeeze through. What makes us bulky?

I believe that things like attachment to the opinions of others, addictions, materialism, pride, greed, anger, holding on to hurts … carrying things like these add weight and girth to us. I believe that we all spend time standing outside the door knowing that we are called to enter but remaining unwilling to let go of some things. Many of us, I think, are squeezing through a little at a time, making wonderful progress by gradually letting go of the things that prevent complete entry into the Lord's Sacred Heart.

A pertinent part of that passage is the Lord's encouraging us to *make every effort.* This tells us that Jesus expects us to cooperate with this process of holiness by relinquishing the things that weigh us down and recommitting daily to the duties of our vocations. We must ask the Lord to help us on each day to let go of our fears and attachments so that we can slip through this door and move into the light of the divine will.

The Sacred Heart of Jesus

"For the Lord takes delight in His people" (Psalms 149-4).

This is so apparent. Jesus experiences each of us as His closest family member. Jesus experiences us as lovable and filled with promise. The experience Jesus has of us is constant and consistent in that He does not check in with us once a week or once a day or even once an hour. The Lord has been with us in a continual and uninterrupted fashion. Jesus never takes His gaze off of us.

Given that He has never been away from us and that He has never stopped considering us, and indeed that He created us, Jesus knows us better than anyone. Jesus knows exactly where we struggle. The Lord understands what we find confusing and where we need greater clarity.

Because His consideration of us has always been, Jesus understands any wounds we carry from our past and how we are living our life because of these wounds. If we are having difficulty as a reaction to woundedness, our Lord is compassionate and seeks to heal us.

Jesus wants to heal us. Our healing is a process which Jesus undertakes personally. Jesus takes the project that is our healing very seriously. Yes, our emotional and spiritual healing is a deeply personal goal for Jesus.

Consider in silence that Jesus is with us now and has been with us for every single moment of our life. He has missed nothing. It is all there in His gaze. We must look at Jesus. We must return His gaze. What do we see in the eyes of our Savior?

There is complete acceptance and compassion in His gaze. We do not have to say one word. Jesus understands everything. His eyes are serious and filled with love for us.

Jesus does not condemn us. This does not come from our beloved Lord. Self-condemnation is planted by our Lord's enemy, who does not want us to accept the Lord's love and heal and then grow in love, taking our intended role in the family of God.

Jesus extends His mercy with the hope that we will understand that in all truth the Lord takes delight in His people.

As the Lord walks through our time on earth with us, His experience of us changes as we change. During some periods, the heart of Jesus is safe with us because we are at peace as a child of God. At other times, there is rebellion and Jesus is hurt by our anger and sinfulness. Does He turn away from us when we hurt Him? Does His heart harden against us?

No.

Consider the love we have for a small child who misbehaves because he is overtired or overstimulated or who has been hurt by a sibling and who then strikes back in outrage. A parent sighs when a child retaliates against another because of anger. Often a parent must lift a kicking and screaming child into his arms and remove him from a situation that has gone wrong and that shows no hope for improvement.

Jesus views our periods of sinfulness in this way. Because He has been with us through each experience, He knows why we behaved badly, if in fact we behaved badly. Our past sins are not viewed as isolated acts but as sins which are often understandable when connected to our pain. Jesus is not harsh. Jesus sees a bad phase for what it is and urges us out of these troubled times. Jesus forgets the past in the interest of the present and the future. We must give Jesus our past and let Him erase our mistakes so that we can rejoice in the present, where Jesus loves us completely.

We must offer ourselves as a safe place for God. Let God

look at us and say, *"Yes, I can count on this apostle to help Me."* Jesus offers us gifts of forgiveness and healing but we must accept these gifts. Let others continue on the path of rebellion and confusion. We will turn sharply now, at this moment, and walk into the Lord's heart completely, where there is mercy and healing. This is the only way for us if we desire heaven.

Jesus will take us to His Father and say, *"Look, Father, there is love for Me on earth. I am welcome in the soul of this apostle."*

This is the right way for us. We must turn away from the world and its shame and walk with Jesus.

September 7, 2007

I see that there are layers inside the place of the divine will. The first is gentleness, then kindness, then generosity of heart, then truthfulness, then eagerness to serve. Those are five. I knew months ago that there were seven so I await the next two.

This is a beautiful work that will require a great deal of contemplation. I see these layers and I understand that they flow into each other in a continuously moving fashion. Apostles existing in the divine will move from one layer to the other, always learning deeper and deeper lessons in each.

I do not see a flat grid of seven layers, but rather a 3-dimensional model, meaning that we drift from one to the next and on and back and in and out. When we are spending time learning gentleness, for example, we remain in that level, working the topic. We enter into what at first appears to be a one-item stop, simple in its instruction. "Be gentle as God is gentle." But then we have to look at each area of our life, each relationship and each moment and apply the lesson of gentleness. This is why it is not a flat model, but a 3-D model with depth and width. The acquisition of each characteristic requires time and transformation in the apostle.

I hear apostles saying, "How do we know if we are in the divine will? Isn't it presumptuous to think that we could rest in such a place?"

Because there are no hard and fast tests on this side of heaven, we will have to look for symptomatic evidence. One symptom for Catholics, to state the obvious, is obedience to the Magisterium of the Church. But I must maintain that for a Catholic, even before this there should be a personal understanding that conformity to the Magisterium of the Church is desirable. If we are not in complete compliance, either in action or spirit, we must ask Jesus to continue His process of moving us along.

Another symptom of being in this place is that an apostle, while perhaps mostly peaceful and content and possessing a generally clear conscience, will not be working every day according to his own will. Most apostles find themselves doing a little something that is repugnant to them. There will be the cross. There are so many reasons for this I will not bother to enumerate them, but will leave it to the Lord as I fear I will go off on a path that leads away from this one. I will sum this up by quoting a man who said about service to Christ, "If it were easy, God could get anyone to do it."

The apostle's experience of existing in the place of the divine will is one of struggle, rather than one of accomplishment. In other words, an apostle serving in the place of the divine will, will look at each layer and think, good heavens, I really need to work on that. The apostle would be right to think this way, but the need for further study and advancement in no way diminishes the fact that the apostle is trying to advance and has indeed made advancements.

The bedrock of this place, this learning place, is obedience to the Church. Obedience will catch us when we, through our fallen natures, rebel against the effort and sacrifice necessary to grow in these heavenly attributes. At times we will need to rest our heads against obedience until our strength has returned. In this instance, when discussing obedience in the context of the bedrock which remains under the place of the divine will, I picture obedience as comforting marble. Some may protest, citing the obvious which is that marble, while possibly beautiful, is hard to the touch. How could this be comforting?

But this firmness is a good thing. Sometimes it is necessary to have something that is immovable. It is not like other surfaces that are malleable and absorb any modern thinking of the day. Marble is solid. The surface that is marble does not change from day to day and neither should our commitment to obedience.

I am simply delighted by this study and find myself fascinated. It is as if God draws us, by the most gracious of invitations, into the secrets of heaven. His generosity astounds me and I rejoice that He allows us to proceed into this study.

September 10, 2007

Today Jesus told me that the sixth layer is prudence.

I see the structure again and recognize it as an area for advanced study in holiness. This is the place where God's children are intended to dwell while they are on earth. Jesus wants each one of us to come to this place and remain in this place. If we remain here, in the place of the divine will, we can be protected. If we remain here, we can be advanced. And, something really important, if we remain here, we can most effectively advance the interests of the Kingdom of God and draw others to Jesus Christ.

Apostles serving in each day must begin to accept that they are chosen. Which apostle is chosen more than another? None. God's choice of each individual apostle is equally complete, equally compelling. Never look at another and think, clearly he is chosen. My call is not like that. It is not as important that I serve in completeness.

And yet, this is the spirit that prowls, seeking to draw God's apostles away from the place of the divine will or preventing them from ever entering the place of the divine will. Consider the author of such a thought. Is it Jesus, telling us that neither our holiness nor our service is important, either to Him personally as our beloved One or to others collectively as our family? No. It is not God who whispers this lie.

Clearly this thought must be abandoned now, dropped outside of the narrow door that invites entrance into the place of the divine will. Let us each pause for a moment and abandon that thought forever.

We are chosen. Rejoice.

The place of the divine will has transparent sides. One is free to look out at other places in the world. This is good, of course, because all that God wills is good. And it is because of this that we can see the unhappy plight of our brothers and sisters who are in sad and unsafe places. But be alert. Do not be one who rests at the outer banks of this place, staring constantly into the world. To do so will cause us distress because we could lose the rhythm of this place and be drawn into the rhythm of other places. Only the rhythm of this place feels right to an apostle. By comparison, other rhythms are discordant and incongruent, leaving God's apostles unsettled and afraid.

Think of a child in the womb. When a doctor puts a listening device against the mother's stomach, a natural rhythm can be detected which is striking in its constancy. The child rests safely in the mother's womb, where he is nourished and comforted in a continual fashion. Would the child seek to exit the womb before the correct time? To do so would be dangerous. Why would the child leave perfect safety?

It is the same way in the place of the divine will. If an apostle looks inward, into his soul, and allows the rhythm of the place of the divine will to advance him in each level of heavenly growth, he will feel contentment.

The source of the rhythm is the beating of the heart of Jesus Christ, which pours uninterrupted graces into those who rest in this place. Will the heart of Jesus Christ ever stop beating? No. We are safe here.

Again, the boundaries of the place of the divine will are transparent, a fact which illustrates the freedom of the apostle to come and go as he wishes. Jesus does not imprison. His invitation to this place originates in His love for us and His desire to protect us.

Despite this truth and given our human nature, there may be times when we feel that our vocation is a prison. We sometimes rail against the place of the divine will, viewing our time there as incarceration. This creates a mystical storm of temptation that is distressing while it lasts. Apostles experiencing this mystical storm must not panic, though. The fact that a storm is raging simply indicates that the struggle is ongoing.

Dear apostles, the struggle will continue while we remain on earth. Periodic mystical storms show that we are holding our swords and doing battle. If we had departed this place, there would be no struggle. This is so important. If we had departed this place, we would be existing in another rhythm altogether.

It is for this reason, the need for struggle, that we must work continually on the concepts of this place because if we work continually, we are less likely to be bounced out of the place of the divine will by our fallen natures during a storm.

In other words, the daily work gives us strength with which to navigate the violence of the storm periods.

We should not be afraid of mystical storms, though they rage on. We are protected by the bedrock, even if there are times when we land so hard on it that we are bruised. It does support us.

Apostles in the divine will have an obligation to provide good examples to each other and to those outside of this place. Because we serve in our humanity, it is true that we will not always set the example that either we or Jesus desires but let us strive to consider always, in our words and actions, what kind of example we are giving to others.

There are some who position themselves around the place of the divine will, never entering, but claiming always to possess the attributes of the Architect of this place. These are the thieves and brigands.

Suddenly, the word hypocrisy springs to mind. We must remember to be authentic.

If we are having a hard time in holiness, we should not try to give the impression that we are worthy of canonization. Now the word humility springs to mind. If we are humble, we are proceeding in truth. We should be humble. To be humble, my friends, is, for lack of a better way of saying it, to *get it*. Others will respect our authenticity and when they witness our efforts they will think, 'Hmm. That must be how it is done.'

Jesus chooses to work with our humanity. Jesus loves us in our humanity. Truly, the Lord takes delight in His people so our struggles give Jesus joy as long as we continue to serve despite them.

September 11, 2007

The last layer, humility, is delightful to consider. I rejoice in the humility of others. I have said before that humility is necessary for holiness. The devil sends humiliation and God turns it into humility. Blessed humility protects us from so many distresses.

I often think that there is an easy way to live and a hard way to live. Working on humility and possessing some humility helps us to proceed along the easy way. Pride takes us on the hard way where everything is a struggle. If we are struggling with pride, we will find ourselves constantly banging against the bedrock. We will be tempted to curse the bedrock at times. We will be tempted to leave the place of the divine will. But we should kiss the bedrock when we land on it as it keeps us in this place.

Jesus is forced to work with a handicap when we are prideful. Do not worry, though. Jesus is used to us.

I am considering the structure of the place of the divine will. When we enter the divine will, we identify it as a place for work in terms of advancing in holiness. Some look at the seven layers and give these things a nod by resting superficially in each. This, in and of itself, is good and hopeful because if we are doing this we are at least identifying the layers. Well done.

There can be hesitation about entering more deeply into each layer because to enter deeply into these layers one must depart from the attributes of the world. It is yet another call to leave something behind and move even further away from it. This is hard work but each apostle must be willing to work.

One moves up the mountain of holiness and into the place of the divine will and then one begins to understand that this place has a depth that moves into the infinity of eternity.

There is no limit, no boundary in the heavenly direction. As we said, there is an outer periphery, which we can call an 'observation deck' which overlooks the world. The study of the Creator is the first priority in the place of the divine will and everything comes from that priority. When you get into the place of the divine will, you must then turn your back to this outer periphery and turn your eyes to God and His heaven.

First, we look at God's plan which we can call Plan A.

Jesus calls us from the world. We climb the mountain. We enter His heart and the place of the divine will. From there we continue the struggle, only we struggle in safety because we are protected by the bedrock from falling down either back onto the mountain or, more seriously, back into the world. Some, after entering the place of the divine will, turn their backs to the world and gaze constantly into infinity, growing steadily into the character and nature of the Creator, moving always more and more deeply into the layers, back further and further toward heaven. These apostles gradually increase in holiness because they accept the graces sent by the Trinity, pumped constantly into this place through the beating of the heart of Jesus. When they die, I suspect they move right past purgatory into heaven, wherein they possess their souls in union with Jesus permanently. Why wouldn't they? Death is simply another advance for them.

This is God's plan for each one of us.

Now we examine another scenario, which we will call plan B. We climb the mountain and enter into the heart of Jesus Christ. We identify the layers and we know that further work and study is necessary in order for us to advance into the character and nature of the Creator. That outer edge, the clear barrier or observation deck draws us, though, and we work for a time, perhaps advancing a little, and then we turn around and see what those in other places outside of the divine will are doing.

In short, we waste time. Something then startles us back into the rhythm and we shake ourselves off and recommit to growth in holiness, thus turning our backs to the world and continuing on His intended journey for us. This happens again and again. We lose the rhythm, find the rhythm, lose the rhythm, find the rhythm.

This, while not God's ideal plan, is acceptable. We are in the holiness game. We are just prone to distraction. This probably describes many of us to greater or lesser degrees.

When we die, we will permanently direct our gaze inward to eternity, of course. This will happen for each person who chooses God. It must. It is best if we fight distraction and do the work here on earth, of course, so we must all strive to move into the Plan A group.

Plan C is another kettle of fish altogether. Plan C people do not seek to enter into the place of the divine will, even though many of them know it is where they eventually want to be. Many are trapped outside the narrow door by the things they are carrying that create bulk. They decide to do this all later. How Jesus yearns to draw them in. Many of us were in the Plan C category and finally slimmed down spiritually enough to enter this place. These are not bad people. We could call them procrastinators.

How does Jesus see the people in this category? Jesus views them with terrific hope. Heaven is not afraid of work and when heaven looks at people in this category, heaven sees a project rather than a failure. We are, each of us, an ongoing heavenly project after all and we are, each of us, called to cooperate with heaven on the projects that are the people around us.

Let me say it this way. When a good mother returns home

to find a messy kitchen, she does not turn around and walk back out of the house, never to return. A good mother simply gets to work, restoring order, accepting that her children will sometimes make messes.

When a mother returns home and the situation is even worse and the kitchen looks like a bomb exploded, she feels even more determined, perhaps eliciting help from some of the older siblings, but again she does not hesitate. There is no question of abandoning the project or allowing the mess to remain. It has to be cleaned.

The souls of the people in the C category are like the children in the messy kitchen. The Church is the good mother. The siblings star as themselves, called into service by the Parent to help restore order to the kitchens or souls of the people in Category C.

People in Category D have rejected God. We pray for them and hope always that their hearts will soften enough to accept His love. We ask God to make us worthy examples of His love. When people in Category D die, they are given a choice. I feel sure that many, confronted with His love, choose Jesus and the family of God.

People in Category E work actively for Satan. I do not know what to say about these. They do not usually admit that they represent the devil. Usually, like the devil, they cloak themselves in a robe like the one that belongs to Jesus Christ. It looks ridiculous on them if you know Jesus at all. Yes, we should pray for their conversion. I am certain that some convert. The hardness of these hearts would chill a holy soul but I feel a strange indifference to them. This indifference is a welcome change from the fear I used to feel when I encountered them.

They have no power over the souls of the just.

September 12, 2007

I am using categories to give some definition to the process and where we are in the process in order to illuminate where we need to go if we are not in the safe place. This is not intended to indict, but to assist in self-evaluation, something that should be ongoing for everyone.

I think many of us move between the first three categories during different periods of our lives. Clearly, Jesus Christ is asking us to get into Category A and stay there so that He can protect us and His goals for us and for the family of God.

It is only necessary to accept God's grace in each given moment. If we do so, we will have exactly what we need to proceed up and in and further back again.

Sometimes I hear people talk about their relationship with the Father. They say, "I go right to the Father." Others feel they do not know the Father but speak only of Jesus. They say, "I have a personal relationship with Jesus Christ."

These relationships are the same in that they are clearly both good and can be complete in and of themselves. In other words, if you are close to Jesus Christ, you are not excluded from being close to His Father or to the Holy Spirit. Indeed, a close relationship with Jesus Christ could not be sustained without the action of the Spirit, who proceeds from the Father and the Son.

I, myself, at one time felt so attached to Jesus that I felt I was neglecting the Father, whom I love most tenderly as much as I am able to in my limited holiness. My initial concern soon melted as I understood that spending time with one, Jesus Christ, did not mean I was neglecting the other, the Father.

A statement often made against Catholicism is that we worship Our Lady and the saints. This is false, of course. We worship the Trinity. This place that I can see helps me to understand far more clearly the fellowship of the Communion of Saints. You see, if the place of the divine will is connected with no separation to heaven, and it is, then the Communion of Saints, those who have triumphed and gone before us, are naturally available to us. Why wouldn't they be? We are all together in this mystical location where we learn about the Trinity, the attributes of the Trinity, and how these attributes became manifest in our brothers and sisters, the saints.

For clarity let me say that when I mention the saints, I am referring to both widely known saints as well as unknown saints. These, the unknown saints, would include those who have gone before us whom we knew and with whom we served. We should consider their lives, the lives of our family members and friends, and rest in the holiness they exhibited by their choices for Christ. It is also good to examine the mistakes they made. They would want us to do this so that we can learn to avoid similar mistakes.

This is not to worship saints, but to study them in the same way a novice golfer might study a highly successful golfer. The novice feels admiration for one who seems to have overcome mediocrity often enough to consistently perform at a high level. This is how we should view the saints. Do we want to be like them? Yes, we should, because they, through their cooperation with grace, achieved holiness, which in essence means they came to resemble Jesus Christ, who perfectly possessed the character of the Father in humanity.

I want to make a distinction for the reader. In order to come to resemble Jesus Christ, we must spend time with others in the place of the divine will. This is fellowship. There are those who are called to work in the world and it is possible that very little holy human fellowship is available to them. They may not have many or any like-minded souls near them in the physical sense.

This should not concern them because if they are in this place, Jesus Christ Himself will determine what fellowship He desires for them. In the absence of human fellowship, they must be disciplined in relying on mystical fellowship, that fellowship that is the prayerful, silent contemplation of God and the saints and angels. My friends, Jesus Christ will often deny a soul human fellowship in order to compel the soul to rely on Him and on the mystical fellowship that comes with Him. Jesus sometimes exhibits a jealous heart, which means that He limits the human influences on a soul in order to give Himself freedom to fashion the soul as He requires and desires. Be at peace in this. If Jesus Christ asks us to work on our soul independently for a time, then that is His prerogative.

When we pass from humanity into eternity, the struggle ceases. While we remain in our humanity, the struggle continues. So, we die and go to heaven and never struggle again. The time for struggle ends. This time on earth, my friends, is a time of the greatest opportunity. We should let nothing stand in the way of holiness but should make holiness and spiritual growth our greatest priority. I am not sure I can communicate this. Let me say it this way.

When we die, we will never regret a decision we made for God or for the welfare of others. We will regret the decisions we made against God and against the welfare of others.

When we die, we will never regret suffering. We will regret violent or rebellious responses to suffering.

When we die, we will never regret a decision to be tolerant of those around us. We will regret decisions to be outraged and intolerant.

This is the tip of the iceberg but the reader no doubt gets the point.

In this line I would like to say that we have certain

standards we adopt as Christians. We aspire to rise to these standards ourselves and we rejoice when others rise to these standards. Humanity being what it is, and life being what it is, we must be flexible, though. We must not allow a Pharisee-like rigidity to poison what is good.

A holy priest recently said that we must accept that some people, because of the circumstances in their lives, compromise. Clearly, if we are holy at all, we will not be concerned about the holiness or, more to the point, the lack of holiness in others, but will remain alert to the need to assist someone who has compromised with standards in order to survive or care for a family. We will also be compassionate to those who compromise because of the pain inflicted on them through the cruelty of others.

This is not to say that we condone sinful behavior, particularly in ourselves. This is to say that we reject rigidity and any judgmental attitude.

⁷ The scribes and the Pharisees were watching him to see if he would cure a man on the Sabbath, hoping to find something to use against him. But he knew their thoughts; and he said to the man with the withered hand, 'Stand up! Come out into the middle.' And he came out and stood there.

⁹ Then Jesus said to them, 'I put it to you: is it against the law on the Sabbath to do good, or to do evil; to save life, or to destroy it?'

¹⁰ Then he looked round at them all and said to the man, 'Stretch out your hand'. He did so, and his hand was better. But they were furious, and began to discuss the best way of dealing with Jesus (Luke 6).

There is so much to learn from this incident. The Pharisees used the law to condemn others rather than to increase their own holiness. Any goodness in Christ was irrelevant to them.

Jesus knew the motives of the Pharisees. He identified the

duplicity of the spirit behind the words and actions and deliberately challenged it. We do not want to be caught in the same way, using our standards as a means to hold ourselves above our brothers and sisters or to try to catch them out. Remember that the enemy of the place of the divine will seeks constantly to present humanity with reasons not to enter into God's safety. We must not let the enemy point to a superior and inconsistent attitude in us as reason why our brothers and sisters should reject God.

This happens all the time, my friends. Let us always be on our guard here. Any apostle could name another who behaves like a Pharisee but that will not be helpful, beyond advancing our understanding of the phenomenon. Jesus would be happier if every apostle scrutinized himself and worked with Him on eradicating any judgmental attitude in the apostle's own soul.

We see that the Pharisees were *looking to condemn.* Remember that this is the opposite of what Jesus did. Jesus looked to save. We must look for evidence of hope and potential in those around us. Some search constantly for evidence of unholiness in others. I think this might be their way of trying to fuel or protect their superiority or obtaining value for themselves in an unhealthy way.

Superiority is something that requires constant feeding, like an addiction. Just as a cigarette smoker needs a nicotine fix periodically, a superiority addict needs to look down on someone periodically. Anyone will do. Those around this type of addict will suffer the most but if the superiority addict must go outside of his inner circle, he is happy to do that. Reading the daily newspaper can work for him in a pinch, but one addicted to superiority will eventually find himself searching for reasons to condemn even the holiest souls.

This should make our skin crawl with revulsion. Really. It

should. I suspect that what is happening is that it is easier to snatch affirmation in small unhealthy doses this way than to actually look within, meet the eyes of Christ and take whatever affirmation we merit in truth while accepting the growth challenges that Jesus puts before us.

I often wonder if these people think they are going to get into heaven by citing the unholiness of others rather than standing on their own holiness. Do they think Jesus will ask them to regale Him with stories about the darkness of the times and the sins committed by those around them? Jesus Christ knows the sins of others and instantly factors in all mitigating and aggravating circumstances in each life. The life we will be accounting for is our own.

Jesus knew the law but He was not rigid because He applied it with love and mercy. Remember that the characteristics of the Trinity include gentleness, kindness, generosity of heart, truthfulness, eagerness to serve, prudence, and humility.

Where do we find these things in the behavior of the Pharisees? Where do we find these things authentically in the behavior of the superiority addicts around us? Look at Jesus in this incident. He, in one situation, exhibits all of the above characteristics. Truly, the smallest bit of contemplation on the earthly actions of Jesus Christ will take the apostle far back into the study of the place that is the divine will.

Again we look at the negative pole in order to intellectually bounce off it and back to the positive.

Did the Pharisees learn from the Lord's example? Did they feel embarrassed at their hostile motives when they were confronted by the truth of the Lord's loving action?

On the contrary, because they were prideful and superior, they felt threatened and enraged by the goodness of Jesus Christ. The Lord's humility and truthfulness, His eagerness to serve by teaching and healing, His gentleness and kindness in showing by example rather than telling by pointing to His own holiness, infuriated them. They refused to take it in because to do so would humble them.

My friends, this is why people choose hell. They are not willing to be humbled.

A superiority addict finds the holiness of others a sour pill to swallow and he will not allow himself to be fed this way. He will choke and spit it out, becoming bitter and angry at the one possessing the goodness of the Lord. What action does superiority prompt?

The Pharisees… began to discuss the best way of dealing with Jesus (Luke 6).

Why do I go on about this? Do I think that apostles do not get it? No, my friends. I go on about this because even the smallest amount of superiority will stunt our growth in holiness. We will be so disappointed in ourselves later if we do not work to eradicate this now. This is an important point to consider for our personal growth and we want to be as holy as we can, but there is another, more compelling reason why I belabor this point.

Apostles behaving in this way are pushing against the renewal. Those in the world, our brothers and sisters living outside of the divine will, will not return if we do not authentically exhibit the characteristics stated above. I know God's mercy and I know that time in purgatory will cleanse us of this superiority, but during this time we have grave need in the world for pure representation of the Trinity.

We must all work on this area. None of us is exempt from a thorough self-examination which seeks to root out feelings of superiority.

Because it is good that we are challenged, I extend this challenge to all apostles. Think of someone who feels superior to you. Then actively try to love him and respond to him with all of the above characteristics.

I want each apostle to know that I am laughing as I write this. I am laughing in delight at the personal revulsion I feel at such a prospect. I am delighted because the thought of the great gaps in my own holiness makes me happy as, if I am identifying the gaps, I know I am seeing myself, with at least some accuracy, as Jesus sees me.

It is human nature to avoid people who behave in this way, of course, but let us, as apostles, think of the Olympics. If we are training for the Olympics, we will look for big challenges. I do not want the apostle who correctly identifies the superiority of another to then fall into the trap of feeling superior to the superior person. His superiority and falseness does not give us cause to abandon the characteristics of the place of the divine will in our dealings with him.

Do you see? It never ends. We step onto a path that we think leads to a short journey and we find, to our possible dismay, that the journey extends far further back than our eye can see. This is our way of proceeding more deeply into this place and this is a great gift to us. When we understand that we are only in the beginning phase of a big, big study, we have obtained the beginning of wisdom.

There will always be a path that extends further back into holiness and we must look for those paths and ask Jesus to help us move along them. If we aim for mediocrity, we may fall short and land in failure. If we aim for exceptional, we are more likely to end up higher than we could ever hope. Jesus does a lot with a little bit of effort on our part but the effort must be consistent.

We must use the law first to become holy and then to save others. Anything else is a misuse or abuse of the law of God.

Sometimes it is good to remember that we are doing battle, not so much with the words and actions of others, but with the spirit that prompts the words and actions.

[12]For it is not against human enemies that we have to struggle, but against the Sovereignties and the Powers who originate the darkness in this world, the spiritual army of evil in the heavens (Ephesians 6).

There are many benefits to remembering this fact.

First, remembering this will help us to understand the moments when we have a strong interior revulsion to statements or actions of others that on their face seem nearly benign. Others will say we are overreacting, perhaps, and yet we know that we are responding to something indiscernible to the worldly mind and heart. A sinister alarm rings in our hearts. We should be calm at this but pay it heed as it could be the Holy Spirit recoiling within us.

Another reason we should remember that our battle is against spirits is that we are then less likely to take things personally. We expect opposition. Every apostle should. We must be adept at shaking off the resistance that presses against us because the fact that we experience resistance in no way changes the work Jesus wills for us. It is not personal and we cannot let attacks distract us.

A third reason to remember this is that we will become less likely to retaliate against the one who comes at us because we can look at him with pity, understanding that he is possibly being used by the opposition to interfere with God's plan. I understand it this way.

I am trying to complete the work that Jesus has assigned to me. If someone assaults me for doing the work God has willed for me, the matter is not so much between me and the aggressor, but between Jesus Christ and His enemy. If I am cut down by darkness Jesus will send someone to take my place. The enemy can attempt to destroy all of God's servants but the enemy will eventually come up against God Himself and the enemy will lose. He has already lost.

I am encouraging every apostle to serve in detachment, remaining anchored in the place of the divine will by a commitment to obedience. The enemy's assaults are an attempt to lure us from this place just as the superiority of another can tempt us to become superior to the superior one. The enemy would love for us to behave like the ones who attack us. This would work against God's plan, of course. We expect those representing the enemy to behave like the enemy. This is no reason or excuse for us to be drawn into such behavior.

We are called to respond like Jesus Christ, our first and best example.

Someone asked me how we should reduce superiority in ourselves. This is a good question.

A daily examination of conscience, our own conscience, is a good place to begin. If we sit down at some stage in each day and ask ourselves where we could have done better in the last twenty-four hours, we will surely come up with some small way to improve in the next twenty-four hours.

Another hint would be to resist comparing ourselves to anyone but Jesus Christ or one of His saints.

I remember a Secular Franciscan saying years ago, "I figure we're doing pretty good compared to most people."

His friend replied, "How do you think we're doing compared to Francis?"

This prompted a great laugh. The man was looking the wrong way in his comparison. Upon consideration, they understood that they were ridiculous to even consider that they were measuring up to the heroic response of St. Francis.

The behavior of Jesus Christ in Scripture is the goal for each apostle. We must always measure against Him.

Another good thing to remember is this fact. We are, in

God's holy truth, not superior. We should accept this and flee from the ridiculousness that accompanies superiority.

We are each different. Our blessings and graces are unique and we are called to respond to the circumstances in our own life and life experience. If we had been given the life experience of another, who is to say where we would be in terms of holiness? I see others who have had extremely difficult lives and yet they are full of goodness and would not knowingly hurt another.

I have seen people who have had no such suffering and yet they fail in love, hurting others regularly with no apology.

We must proceed in the truth which is that we have work to do in our souls. Jesus judges. Only He has all of the information necessary to do so.

To recap something important, we can fight superiority by examining our conscience daily, measuring only against Jesus Christ or one of His saints, and reminding ourselves of the truth, which is that we are not superior. Humility is absolutely necessary for holiness.

As a warning, I am not encouraging a harsh treatment of self. I remember telling someone that he was awfully hard on others. He said, "Yes, but I am hard on myself, too." This statement was made as if to say, "I can condemn others because I condemn myself."

I said, "Jesus is just as displeased with your self-condemnation as He is with your condemnation of others."

A good apostle will apply the kindness of Christ to himself as well as others.

It seems to me that the children have been turned against the mother. Many Catholics see themselves as separated from the Church, even exhibiting anger and rebelliousness against the Church. They make statements like this:

"The Church is only after money. All priests are pedophiles.

The Church is all about rules."

Let me translate these statements in order and try to guess what is really meant.

"I don't want to give away any of **my** money. I can use pedophilia as an **excuse** not to go to Church. I personally do not **want** to obey God's rules."

Clearly, some claiming to represent the Church have made mistakes and committed sins and abuses. The enemy tempted them efficiently and, for whatever reasons, they were not armed against the temptations. The ones abandoning God's path allowed many to be lured out of safety through their actions.

But I ask each person to look at the Church. If one studies the Church, one will see that Her guidelines are protective in nature, most priests serve ably and truthfully, and each Catholic should, if possible, give some money so that the individual parishes can be maintained and so that the wider goals of the Church can be achieved.

If the Church flourished financially in one period, rejoice. If there are those who then squandered the Church's assets through either criminal behavior or fiscal irresponsibility, God will hold them accountable. It is still no reason for us to abandon the Church, and a financially poorer Church will not do us any harm at all.

We must think of Jesus Christ when we think of the Church. What does He need us to do to help raise up the Church? Again, to repeat a point almost to tiredness, the misbehavior of some is no excuse for others to abandon God's cause in the Catholic Church.

September 17, 2007

One obvious difficulty for humanity is accepting that Jesus

is present both in the human experience as well as in the mystical experience. The Lord our God is with us on both levels, continually, and, if allowed, uses each human experience to provide growth for the soul. An apostle cooperates in this by accepting and welcoming Jesus into both experiences, in other words, into the reality that is the present moment on earth.

I have heard many priests urging people to allow Jesus into their lives. I remember one priest, during a homily, commenting on the good manners of everyone in the church. He said, "I want to see these same good manners in the parking lot when Mass is over." He was identifying the fact that we often do not allow for the presence of Christ in our everyday life.

It is true that some of the time the experience of our humanity is that of loneliness and pain, discouragement and sadness, and above all, isolation, even from those closest to us. It is said that every man is an island and I believe that there is truth to this. Still, I think God requires periodic isolation in order to fix each man's eyes more firmly on Him. Some lessons we must learn alone. Period. Humanity cannot breach this type of isolation.

If we accept that feeling abandoned in our pain and feeling that nobody understands our pain is necessary for us to grow in holiness, we will be less afraid of these periods. We will lament less. We should view these times as invitations from the Trinity to rest our souls in the place of the divine will, where we are surrounded by saints and angels.

I hear sighs from others, even as I sigh myself. We are all thinking, if it were only that easy. How do we do this?

The only way I can think of is through trust. We trust that Jesus is with us. We trust that He allows us to experience whatever pain is occurring in order to advance our soul. We trust that we are in a safe place in the heart of Jesus. We trust that there are no separations and that we have access to a vast number of heavenly companions. We trust that God has a plan for us and that He will not abandon us to the whims of the devil even though our humanity looks out and sees enemies all around us. We trust that we know only the barest tip of the power of the Father.

Trust, trust, and more trust will help us to accept that we, during times of darkness, may be faltering in our humanity but making magnificent gains in our spirituality. Our failures, when acknowledged and regretted, can only make us holier if we trust in the Lord's merciful presence with us, even in failure.

I must reference an experience I had of heaven where Jesus asked me to view a former time of my life and see it from heaven's perspective. My first reaction was, *I would not want to live that period again. It was very hard.* Apostles, please know that I was tempted to write *It was too hard* but found that I could not as when I viewed it from heaven's perspective, it was evident that it was not *too hard*, but hard. *Too hard* would mean that I could not possibly have navigated the time. Clearly, viewing it with Jesus, I could see that while it was difficult, the graces sent by heaven made it manageable.

That experience is what I am thinking of when I examine the distinction between the experience of the human being and the soul. I suffered significantly in my humanity and, at the same time, my soul advanced in a spectacular fashion. But this spectacular growth could only be seen from heaven. Such detachment growth! It was impressive to see what heaven accomplished while I suffered.

The more time we spend in silence, contemplating God's Kingdom and acknowledging our soul, the less likely we will be to panic when we feel abandoned in the periodic anguish of our humanity.

I am very aware of this in terms of others. I see people suffering all around me. I know their pain is great when it comes to concern for loved ones. I understand the temptation to think that all is lost or that a loved one will never return to wellness or holiness. How many of us suffer because of the separation of family members from God? How many of us suffer aching helplessness as loved ones flounder?

Again I return to trust. We, as apostles, rest in the promise that if we look after the Lord's interests, He will look after ours. We should carry that promise with us everywhere, most particularly when we watch those around us suffering and when those around us hurt us. Jesus will use every experience for good, both for us and for others.

I think that we spend our time on earth climbing the mountain of holiness and coming in and out of the place of the divine will. The goal is to spend all of our time in this place, of course, or, we could say, to stay in place.

Mystical Storms

September 20, 2007

Jesus was tempted in the desert for forty days. Imagine. Such a penitential forty days that must have been. Surely Jesus must have used every holy strategy available to combat the fatigue, the physical weakness and the discouragement.

We also face difficult times, though not to the same extent. There are certain periods an apostle encounters that we can think of as mystical storms. This is when everything looks normal from the outside, but on the inside we are doing terrific battle.

One type of mystical storm is the mystical storm of temptation. We experience this when we look at our life and we feel rebellious and angry. Everything we look at inspires us to bitterness. In mild form, this is manageable and we could call it discouragement. In severe form, we are tempted to abandon the work the Lord has designed for us. Oh my, we have all been in the firing line of someone close to us who is experiencing a mystical storm of temptation. It is not pretty.

When someone close to us is experiencing this, the statement "Don't take it personally" is very important.

Consolation, when it comes, slips through the sufferer's fingers like sand, even as we try to hang on to it. The enemy rants tirelessly, convincing us that our service is fruitless and that our offerings are like so much rubbish. Any holiness we possess seems to disappear and we have no recall of our past service or spiritual triumphs. We forget all evidence of the Lord's providence.

It's a bit like being on a merry-go-round that is broken and revolving at such a speed that reality is a blur. Our mystical vision lights on something for a moment but we grasp only the injustice of the thing before we are speeded away, onto the next thought. It is like the enemy is hiding behind a tree shooting poison darts at us. We don't see him but we feel the darts as they pierce us with poison, a poison which seems to befoul all that is good.

It sometimes feels as though we are swimming and suddenly pulled under water from beneath. I think the predominant feelings are bitterness and anger and the temptation will always involve a rebellious alteration of the course that the Lord has laid out for us in our service and vocation.

During this time the enemy tempts us in many ways, most particularly in ways we are vulnerable. How many of us have had the complacency to scoff at an obvious temptation, only to be levelled shortly after by something more sly. Surely the enemy gloats but that is okay. We accept periodic sin and failure as part of our humanity.

Later, when it ends, we can see the ridiculousness of the more extreme temptations, but even in the ridiculousness there is no place for laughter. The enemy is sinister and it takes some time to recover from this mystical storm of temptation.

Jesus allows these things for us, just as He accepted these temptations during His time on earth. The key is this. We must never depart from our prayer disciplines or our duties during these periods. If we hold firm on prayer and service, we insulate the Lord's plan. These periods have the potential for damage but we ask Jesus each day to protect His plan from our weaknesses.

As I have said before, Jesus can lift the influence from one moment to the next. There is hope.

Another type of mystical storm is one of separation. During this painful storm we feel terrible grief and sadness, as though someone has died. Anything that formerly gave us joy seems horridly flat and our service and life seems to stretch out tediously before us. A person suffering through this storm may find himself doing mathematics, examining his current age against the normal life span of others and wondering when Jesus will come for him.

Great guilt follows these mental meanderings as which one of us would wish to abandon our loved ones and duties or wish to bail out of the Lord's service simply because we are homesick for heaven?

My friends, as with the previous type of storm and the storm I will describe next, it is often only the observation of a friend that can clarify this experience for the sufferer. Most are unable to identify this storm, though, even for another. It is heaven that usually illuminates this for a person.

This storm is one of longing and pain. It can be most closely identified with the pain of a grievous heart break. Grief pops up like popcorn, at random times, and the sufferer feels vulnerable and close to tears, but also conversely invulnerable in that nothing could hurt him worse than the pain in his heart at being denied union with Jesus. Think in terms of sorrowful, aching, hurting, sadness.

In the same way that we experience a mystical storm of separation from Christ, we can experience a mystical storm of separation from Christ present in the soul of a brother or sister. This occurs when we are allowed to experience Christ's presence within the soul of a brother or sister to a degree that delights us. This delight quickly turns to pain, though, because we are as limited in our ability to fully experience Christ in the soul of our brother or sister as we are in our ability to experience Christ Himself fully while we remain in our humanity. This is another sweet pain, of course, and while we would not desire to relinquish it, we do experience suffering from it.

One feels bemused at the extent of these anguishes of separation. Speech is without value here as the pain cannot be quantified or identified. I wonder at the wisdom of attempting to describe this at all and yet I believe it will be infinitely helpful to someone suffering in this way. Here is my best advice.

One should not feel guilt. One is not looking to abandon his ship of service simply because one wishes he were already permanently united to either the Communion of Saints or our beloved Jesus. There will be no **serious** temptation to take one's life. One simply longs for Jesus. This is no sin. This hurts and Jesus understands the hurt of the separation but allows the pain for His greater glory.

Imagine our Blessed Mother after Jesus died! Surely the remainder of her life must have been dominated by one long mystical storm of separation.

One should keep telling oneself that the pain will end. We will have our Jesus. We will spend eternity with Him and with the whole Communion of Saints. Even this mystical storm will pass and the weight of the cross of separation will again become more manageable. Isn't Jesus wonderful that separation from Him causes such grief? One day we will rest our heads against His chest as John did and tell Him all about this pain.

I know that I need to write that Jesus is not separated from us in reality. He is always with us. I know that I need to write that because it is true and yet I also know that the person experiencing this mystical storm will not be consoled by this fact because the anguish of the separation is such that this fact does not pierce it. Still, it must be said that, in truth, Jesus never abandons us.

I think something that might comfort sufferers of the

mystical storm of separation is this. In heaven, each will have complete possession of that which he seeks and that which he longs for. The longing will cease and we will have total fulfillment of our craving for Jesus and the truth that He brings with Him. Rejoice. It will come. We do not offend the Lord in our pain, but give Him great glory. Serve on. There is most certainly a finish line.

One final observation is that the grief of separation is the smallest, most miniscule indication of the joy we will feel at reunion.

The next mystical storm is the mystical storm of doubt. In this storm, all confidence is removed. Self-esteem plummets. Nothing is beyond the reach of our doubts. We doubt our holiness, our service, the fruits of our service, we doubt the commitment of others, the success of our holiness struggle, we doubt our motives. We doubt the Lord's presence in our work, we doubt that the saints are really helping us or connected to us. We doubt that angels are intervening and assisting, we may doubt the existence of heaven and purgatory, we doubt ultimate justice, eternal salvation, and perhaps even the existence of God.

I remember a story about Mother Teresa of Calcutta who looked at the Eucharist and asked someone, "What is that?" The person told her and she was consoled. She knew what it was but she was probably experiencing a fierce mystical storm of doubt. During this period, one is tempted to believe that one has no faith, which creates the inevitable guilt.

A person experiencing this recently made such a statement. The person with whom she spoke said, "What is faith?"

Well, that was a very good question to the sufferer as she was not sure but answered, "Belief in God."

The person then said, "You made a decision to serve God in the past because you believed in God and today, despite your doubts, you got up and served God. You have plenty of faith."

In this storm, the sufferer loses the horizon. It is as if a cloud covers the North Star and the sufferer becomes disoriented. In extreme cases, everything goes upside down and what seemed right now seems wrong and what seemed wrong now appears to be worth considering. There is sadness in this, too, the feeling of having lost something or having had something taken away. One looks at those around him who are not suffering the mystical storm of doubt and one wonders why they are so sure and confident in their service. Oh my, how we suffer during this period. In its mildest form, there is a little uncertainty. In its most virulent form, one is absolutely terrified.

With regard to all three mystical storms, one must remember that they can overlap or join in places and a perfect storm will encompass some elements of all three. There is usually a prevalent theme to a storm, however, with one of the three, temptation, separation, or doubt being most apparent.

The separation storm is so sad because one believes in Jesus to the point of agony but one feels one cannot be with Him. I am reverent at the pain of this suffering.

Remember, these are finite periods of suffering that Jesus can end with a glance.

Great spiritual growth is achieved through each period.

One is only at risk in the storm if one alters his service or prayer disciplines.

September 21, 2007

Heaven surrounds the storm victim with protection.

Others probably will not understand the extent of the

suffering. Be at peace. Heaven understands.

Because we are called to advance into the characteristics of the Father, it will be helpful to examine each one. As I said, God desired to assist us in acquiring His image and likeness, so He sent Jesus in order to show us exactly how the image and likeness looked in human form. What a blessing.

How difficult for us now to claim we did not understand.

God can point to Jesus Christ and respond, **Oh yes you did.**

The Father is gentle and Jesus, having come from the Father and possessing all that is in the Father, is also gentle.

Jesus is gentle in the way He both encourages and corrects.

If a person is doing well, Jesus does not send marching bands to applaud the progress. He simply continues to accompany the person, sending a stream of peace and calm. Words are unnecessary when God's peace and calm surrounds one. When Jesus wills that a soul be given greater illumination of things divine, He illuminates gently. The soul is not alarmed or frightened, rather his gaze is directed to an area he formerly could not see or understand. Suddenly, what was invisible and indistinct now becomes visible and clear. God's encouragement does not startle. It feels natural, so much so that the soul can miss these gains if he is not paying attention in silence each day.

Jesus is gentle in the way He corrects. The Lord never seeks to hurt for the sake of hurting. Jesus allows necessary pain, of course, but He sends all manner of graces to comfort and console.

Many will recall the sudden death of a family member. Such stunning shock! Many also will recall the tremendous graces surrounding the shock and many will say, truly, with great conviction, "The Lord was in it."

Of course the Lord was in it as He does not abandon His

beloved ones when they suffer.

Now in the case of necessary reprimands, Jesus also moves gently. He whispers to the soul who places himself in silence and who truly seeks the light of Christ. The Lord gently illuminates an area of mistake or a departure from the path. Picture a dimmer light switch being turned up ever so slowly.

We may have suspected we were at fault. On some level we knew we were behaving in a manner inconsistent with the true call to behave like Christ. Jesus needs us to see this. He needs to identify our erroneous actions or thinking and He does so in silence, gently, but seriously.

When I say He corrects gently, I want to communicate that the Lord is never spiteful and He never gloats at our mistakes or sins. He never says gleefully, "Got you." He does not lie in wait to catch us sinning, like the Pharisees did to Him.

Rather He stands alongside the path to prevent us from wandering away. When we wander, He follows, wherever we go, waiting to illuminate for us the condition of our soul in His light of truth. Jesus loves us. Our sinfulness saddens Him but He will never strike out violently against us.

Now it must be said that one of the greatest graces Jesus allows is sudden conversion. These St. Paul-like experiences must be the delight of the saints in heaven. I believe Jesus does this when He needs service from the person NOW. He perhaps has tried to shift the soul gently but the soul is stubborn in his resisting the plan of our beautiful Jesus.

This, my friends, I believe to be the most loving of actions. A soul bounced from his horse, metaphorically speaking, surely can have no doubt that his service is of urgent importance to the Kingdom and his resistance is doing damage to the Kingdom. Clearly, the humble soul rests in the latter thought.

Even in situations like this, there is evidence of the Lord's gentleness. Jesus surrounds the soul with grace, sending in help from both heavenly and earthly sources. The soul is guided very carefully afterwards into the service intended for him.

I think that a soul experiencing the Lord's correction abruptly will sometimes not feel that it happened gently in terms of the impact it has on his life. Here is why.

When someone turns on the lights suddenly and a person sees the error or falseness in which he has been living, that person might be tempted to run for cover. My friends, this feeling of being exposed is inevitable.

2Everything that is now covered will be uncovered, and everything now hidden will be made clear. 3 For this reason, whatever you have said in the dark will be heard in the daylight, and what you have whispered in hidden places will be proclaimed on the housetops (Luke 12).

Again, I say, do this now. We must ask Jesus to show us any areas where we can improve ourselves and then we will have no unpleasant surprises when we die. Jesus will be gentle in showing us the wrong way and the right way. Once we ask forgiveness, acknowledging our error, Jesus simply draws us into the correct course. We must face forward and not let the enemy try to force us to look constantly at any mistakes we have made.

I want to say that as we see Jesus drawing us forward, away from our sin, we see the enemy, forever reminding us of our sins and trying to persuade us that we cannot serve effectively because of past mistakes. I have said it is like the enemy paints our sins on a billboard and then follows us, constantly holding this billboard of our sins in front of us. This is annoying, it is true. Always remember that this is a distraction which comes from Satan, not God.

Part Two

Visions

April 30, 2007

The Lord brought me to Him on a hillside that overlooks the earth. I saw the earth turning. Over many regions hung clouds of black smog and darkness, which I understood to be generated through hard hearts and sinfulness. I am talking about anti-God sentiments and behaviors. I could see that some regions were badly affected and the smog from these areas spread out to other parts of the world. Jesus brought my attention to the risk that if there is enough of this, the earth will be covered, entombed by this darkness. Many of His children will be cut off from heaven's light if this were to happen. Jesus does not will this darkness of sin to cover and entomb the earth at this time. He is intervening.

I wondered about the efforts of the apostles serving in these areas because I could sense the terribly fierce battles taking place under these clouds. It was as if I could hear the clash of swords. Jesus said that in some areas, sin had been overcome and the production of this evil had been arrested through the efforts of apostles who have fought the good fight. These areas have been purified. God is so pleased with these successes for heaven. For whatever reason, though, in other areas the apostles are in need of help.

I saw Jesus lower His hand and wipe it across one of the areas in the sky above the earth. In one wave, He gathered all of the blackness in that area and closed His hand. When He closed His hand, the blackness and filth disappeared. The area was purified. I looked down at the earth where heaven now filled it with light. It looked like it had been affected. In worldly terms, it looked like it had been affected badly, but in heavenly terms I knew that God had intervened and prevented the constant flow of darkness that this area had generated. He cut off the ability of the enemy to work here.

This is a joy to the apostles serving here and they are heaven's soldiers and will be rewarded as such.

I asked Jesus what He would say to those who fight on for Him in areas where the fierce battle is being waged. He said, **"They must fight the fight with great love and even greater humility."**

This is God's mercy, His plan. We are a part of His plan and another part of His plan is that He will intervene. His countenance is serious but not angry. I must say that what springs into my head is that the sin of abortion is contributing to a great production of this heavy and dense blackness. We cannot kill God's children and think it will be a course acceptable to the Father. I am acutely aware that this is my thought but I am speaking honestly about what came into my head at the view of the darkness.

In many areas there is some smog but more heavenly light, the light that comes from God's servants there. God purifies these areas in ongoing fashion. In the high-problem areas at this time, the apostles cannot keep up because there are so few serving and the sins are so serious and numerous.

The Lord is asking me to record my feelings about this vision. I feel nothing. It is the Lord's affair. We are all here on earth temporarily, so to grieve those taken in any purification would be to grieve those taken with cancer, heart disease, or old age. If the Lord wills that it is time, it is time.

May 1, 2007

Yesterday, I began by praying to the Father. He told me that the first thing I needed to do was to go to Jesus and then record what I experienced. Jesus drew me back to Himself on the hillside. He told me that I was in the special position of being able to ask Him questions about the things that I am being shown and that He wanted me to take advantage of this and ask Him any questions I had.

I looked at the world and remembered yesterday's vision of the way the Lord simply swept the blackness away with a wave of His hand. From this perspective, heaven's, it is so simple and right. I understand that the Lord's heart is one of perfect purity of motive. He knows what He is doing and why and how it will benefit humanity. I am not inclined to ask Him anything but understand that it is my humanity that the Lord is using so I did ask Him this question:

"Lord, from here it looks so simple and clear but I understand and have seen that from the earth the experience is profoundly different. On the ground, in the midst of upheaval, there is anguish and suffering and terrible shock. People grieve and suffer the greatest emotional distress. Jesus, what would You say to them?"

Jesus replied, *"Anne, consider a patient who requires surgery. He is ill. Because the person is not a doctor, he may not understand the extent of his illness. A doctor makes a decision that surgery is necessary for both the immediate and future health of the patient. Consider how a person feels immediately after the surgery. Often after surgery, a patient feels shock and pain. He must rest and recover. With proper care, he then begins a process back to wellness. His condition is improved. The surgery was deemed necessary by one who understood the condition of the patient.*

In the situation you observed yesterday, I am the doctor. I can see that My children are unwell and failing to flourish. Because of My divinity, I can see that if they are allowed to proceed on the course in front of them, they will suffer even greater distress in the future. For this reason, I allow this purification. In the immediate aftermath, there is suffering and distress, it is true, but My grace is present and with My divine care and heavenly nursing, My children will be restored to purity and joy. Anne, I act only in the best interests of the children of God. To do otherwise would be impossible for Me and you know this. In the days to come, you must consider other questions that My children would like to ask Me."

May 2, 2007

Today I sat with Jesus on the hillside. After a short time, Jesus rose and asked me to come with Him. We were in a different place, but a place where I had been before. We were in a forest in heaven and, for a moment, I sat on one large stone seat and Jesus sat on another. I listened for a while to the sounds. I heard many different types of birds and this was very happy for me. I looked up and saw tall trees all around us. Jesus asked me if I had questions for Him.

I thought of one that was posed to me and I asked Jesus whether He willed actions or allowed them. Jesus said, to paraphrase, that if an action committed by man was prompted by God, committed in good will and with good intention, then we should accept that God willed the action and result. If an action is committed by man but prompted by God's enemy, committed with bad will and malice, then we should accept that God allowed the action, honoring His gift of free will, but that it was not God's will. In other words, this is not the way the Lord would have chosen that the situation unfold.

I digested this and thought of another set of circumstances. I asked Jesus about a situation that was prompted by good intention, with good will, but that ended in tragedy. Was this God's will or did God allow it? Far from being impatient with me, Jesus was patient in the extreme. For private purposes, I have to admit that I was thinking of a situation where someone goes out in a boat in an attempt to rescue another and runs over him instead, killing him. The motive was pure, the intention good. Is this God's will or did God allow it?

Jesus said, *"Anne, this is what the world would consider a tragedy. Evil did not prompt the person to injure the victim. It is what is called an accident in earthly terms. Is it My will for this person to return to Me at that time? Yes. It is My will. You are thinking of another case, the case in which a child dies. Ask Me that question."*

I asked the Lord about the difference between a child going to heaven and a priest going to heaven. The priest served a long life, brought others to God, no doubt fought many battles against himself and for others. He lived a process of knowing God, entering deeper and deeper into God. The boy, on the other hand, did not have an opportunity to know God in the same way. Clearly, he was not given the chance to advance far, to fight these battles, to overcome himself over a period of time. I asked Jesus about the eternity of the priest as compared to the boy.

I turned my head and saw a boy. I would recognize him again if I saw him today on the street. Jesus told me that this boy is a fully mature being of God. The boy began to talk and explained these things to me. He said that he was given the same opportunities to move into the life of the Trinity in eternity as the priest. This boy spoke to me as a mature saint. The boy explained to me that the priest would be given honor in heaven, as all saints who choose unity with Christ on earth are given honor. He said that most people do not choose this until death in that they do not decide to work exclusively for Jesus in their hearts. Priests make a decision to do this on earth and we all rejoice in their decision and accomplishments in heaven. I used the example of the priest because that was the comparison that came to my mind. A woman serving would be the same, of course, except she obviously does not share in the divine priesthood. The priesthood is unique and a priest's eternity will also be unique to his cooperation with heaven in the Lord's priesthood.

This young man spoke with total confidence and knowledge. He had such wisdom and he was so kind to me. He said that what is important is the desire to know God. He, in his short life, desired to know God, particularly at the end when it was clear to him that God was taking him home. While he did not have the opportunity to fight the great battles against himself, he had little impurity to influence him and had no cause to fight these battles. You might say God spared him these battles as God had no need for him to be perfected in this way. God's will for him on earth was completed at the moment of his death.

I next thought of a tragedy that caused a child to suffer terribly and then die. Is this God's will? Or does God allow it?

Jesus said, **"I often will suffering for my children on earth as My Father willed suffering for Me. In suffering, great purification and growth can occur. Anne, little dove, in the suffering of a child who suffers as I suffered, innocently, many can be drawn to Me. You will often see great spiritual advances in the people around a suffering child. When any one person is suffering on earth, you** *can be sure that there is opportunity for holiness present for others. It is My will that My children assist each other. Do not become angry because there is suffering. Become committed to Me and help to ease or eradicate the suffering of others, if only through prayer for them.*

How did I deal with the suffering of others? I took time to listen to the sufferings of those around Me. I healed them when it was the will of the Father. You, too, should ask the Father to heal others. You should listen to their pains and anguishes. You should ask Me about My will for you in the suffering of others. At no time should you believe that I have abandoned anyone who suffers. I am there. I am with the suffering one and I am with those around the one who suffers and there are lessons for every person in every circumstance."

I thought of earthquakes. I asked Jesus if He willed earthquakes. He said that God, as the Creator, is the only one who knows each detail of the earth's qualities and only He knows exactly why each thing happens in the earth, on the earth and above the earth. Does He will an earthquake? Yes, in the respect that He knows exactly what the earth will do as it moves through its period of existence. Changes come and God knows about them in advance. I got the feeling that while we do not always understand why such a thing is allowed by God, it is allowed by God and it is willed by God if it comes from nature. We can hardly thank Him that the sun comes up each day and then object when the tide rises. If the earth shifts and a tsunami occurs, taking lives, we must accept that the earth shifted and a wave resulted and some of our brothers and sisters are finished here but we are not.

When Jesus spoke, He spoke with perfect clarity.

I do believe, based on this experience, that God wills all events that come from nature, short of those that occur when nature is manipulated unnaturally. In those cases, God allows the outcome out of respect for the gift of free will given to man.

May 3, 2007

Today the Lord brought me to another place in heaven, again, a place where I have been before. It was the waterfall. I sat alongside the stream with Jesus, where the water runs past, out from the pool. I understood that the Lord wanted me to enjoy myself so I watched as others, visible to me as lights unless I wanted to engage them, rejoiced in the water. I looked at the light flowing in and out of each drop of water. The water reflected the light and created a prism through which the light moved. I am at peace that there is no way to describe this and do it justice. It is part of God's active participation in all created things and these souls in heaven are experiencing the greatest wonder and joy in all of it. There was warmth in the sun, coolness in the water, and reverence in God's presence. It was all joyful.

Jesus told me that He wanted to show me a glimpse of people on the earth before the renewal and after the renewal. Jesus then brought me back to the hillside and I looked at the earth.

I saw a woman on a bus. She looked disheartened. She gazed out the window, seeing nothing. She seemed sad and unloved. I knew she was married but I also knew that there was no free exchange of love between this husband and wife. In front of her, inches from her eyes really, drops of rain rolled down the window. The sun was out and the light reflected through the drops of rain in a beautiful manner. It was the same as in the heavenly waterfall except for one difference. She could not see God's presence. She was not open to the experience of God's love in His created things. God loves this woman so much and she is a good woman who loves God but she does not understand His presence. One would really want to comfort her.

I next saw a man working in a place of construction. He also looked disheartened. He was standing next to a drain down from which water flowed. The sun was shining and I saw the light glistening from points in the water. The water looked like diamonds shining and the movement of the light created the effect of diamonds all over, here, then there, always moving and shifting. It was like a joyful dance of light through water. This man felt a spark of childlike joy, an urge to laugh aloud and to splash at the water to see the change. What would the light do if he splashed it? How would the picture change? How would it be after a splash of movement? I saw a glimpse of God's heavenly joy in his eyes. For a moment he looked very happy and years younger. Then it left and he looked disheartened again but he stared at the water and he knew, in some way, that God was with him and that he was loved.

Next I saw a religious sister, darker skinned than I am. She wore a habit with a rounded veil. She was cleaning outside near a fountain in a warm climate. The fountain had tiers and water flowed down from one level onto the next. The sun was shining and this sister had a joyful countenance. In her hands she held garbage that she was picking up and I saw her turn to the fountain to pick something up there. When she bent down she looked up at the water flowing into the larger pool at the base and she noticed the light moving through the water and off the water as it fell. She seemed mesmerized.

"God, you want to play with me and I have work to do," she said aloud in a teasing voice. She thanked God for His presence and moved into her work again with such joy. She appeared very young but when I looked closely at her I could see that she was not young in years. It was her spirit that was open to God and God's love moved freely into her soul. This woman went along with her business with great love in her and this love flowed from her to others. Her smile was beautiful to see.

Jesus said, *"Anne, you have been given a glimpse of the fruit that will come from the renewal. After being renewed, the first two will proceed in the same way as My beloved Sister Annunciata. Consider that in the future, when the first two see these things, they will rejoice as this religious sister rejoiced and their souls will participate in an open exchange of love with Me. They will know they are loved and they will accept My love, which will then flow through them to others, despite any difficulties in their daily lives. Work tirelessly for the renewal because through it I bring joy to My children who feel unloved."*

September 24, 2007

Today Jesus showed me the mountain of holiness. Near the top I saw an area that I knew to be the entry to the divine will, the heart of Jesus. I understood that some identify this as the right goal for them and they work hard to climb the mountain and enter into the narrow door. They do so and begin the work of acquiring the image and likeness of God. This work is difficult, of course, and at times, through our fallen natures, we are drawn to the side that faces the world.

The necessary formula for advancing is simple and I have stated it before. We must say no to self and yes to God.

I saw a man drawn to the side that faces the world and he began to look with envy on the acclaim that others were receiving. He lost the rhythm and stepped out of the place of the divine will. His mystical countenance changed and I could see that while he mimicked the ones there, his soul was no longer reflective of the characteristics of either God or those who remained in the place of the divine will, working on their souls. I actually saw bitterness and disdain in his face when he looked at those remaining.

I saw this person suspended for a moment and I said, "Jesus, what is supporting him?"

Jesus said, *"Nothing."*

The man fell down to the mountain. The only way back to the place of the divine will was to climb again and enter through the heart of the Lord. I understood that some fell back down onto the mountain, some fell all the way down to the ring of defiance, and some continued on into the world and beyond.

I said, "Jesus, how far will this man go? Will he go all the way back into the world?"

Jesus directed my vision to the area of the fallen-aways and beyond, into the group that works for the enemy and I saw some who had once been in the place of the divine will but who now worked with the enemy. This was terribly disturbing for a moment but then I realized that truth is truth and God is still God and I was not as disturbed. God sends grace.

I saw people falling down in the place of the divine will but landing on obedience. I saw some disobeying and falling out of the place of the divine will but only for a short time as they immediately re-entered through the Lord's heart. This was not a dangerous matter. It is different from the first man in this way.

The first man rejected God's will in order to gain the worldly things he craved: acclaim, material things, power. The second person was not willing to reject God, even though he behaved badly and made trouble for others.

The person who does not leave obedience, either in spirit or action, is not at risk. The bedrock of obedience supports him and he goes straight from the bedrock of obedience back into the work because he is willing to admit fault and repent. Remaining in error through pride will draw one backwards on the mountain.

The person rejecting the divine will, nourishing hatred for what is good, is at risk.

I think a superiority addict can fall into both categories, the latter being more sinister, of course.

Jesus showed me this vision so that we can be alert. Jesus wants us to be vigilant about our holiness and our commitment to staying in the place of the divine will.

Later, I was musing about this and saw the man who had left the place of the divine will. He was, in truth, not very far along on the mountain, however he projected his image up to the holy place, presenting himself to others as though he were saintly. I saw Jesus look at him and the man feebly tried to point to the image of himself high in holiness. Jesus looked right past the man's representation of himself, into the man's soul and dealt with the man in truth. This was not easy for the man.

September 25, 2007

Today Jesus brought me to the top of the mountain. From this vantage point, above the mountain, I could see many climbers and this was a happy site. Toward the top I understood that Jesus was drawing people in through His Sacred Heart. People were softened here and, in terms of their self-will, very compliant and easy for Jesus to draw. They moved naturally into the place of the divine will. Jesus brought me in and I understood many things.

I saw today that some re-enter time and time again because they are drawn back into the world time and time again. This is okay in terms of their desire to be with the Lord and the Father, but they are precluded from making and retaining gains in the seven characteristics because they do not stay at any one lesson long enough to master it, as much as we can master it here on earth.

I saw others making real gains in these Godly traits. As they advanced further into the divine will, back and up toward heaven, I saw the place of purgation and understood why holy ones need not stop there. They have grown enough in holiness where they accept God as Father and themselves in their flawed humanity and there is no further need for purification. They possess the traits.

I saw others who came from the place of the divine will but required further self-acceptance and understanding of their flawed humanity and they were drawn to the place of purgation. Either way is fine in terms of the final outcome but souls will be glad if they give Jesus effort in holiness here. This is a huge understatement that each reader must spend time with as words will not communicate this concept with any adequacy. Some things can only be communicated with grace.

Given this vision, I have a better understanding of why the Church has always sought to assist dying people. It is best for people to be in the divine will at death. If they are, there is no need for that terrible moment when they face the Lord and He says, *"Which do you choose?"* They will not require this if they are in the state of grace. They will simply move from life to eternity along the only possible path for them. It is all very natural and right. Again I say that we should have no fear of this process.

There is an opening that leads to heaven and this vision is consistent with what I saw years ago when I saw someone drawn from purgatory into heaven.

To clarify, purgatory is connected to the Kingdom of God. Based on seeing its location today, I understand more fully why Jesus said that **"A vast eternity separates the two"** meaning purgatory and hell. Purgatory is part of the Heavenly Kingdom and hell has nothing to do with purgatory.

Also, Jesus draws people into His Sacred Heart with a powerful magnetic love that is stronger than all malice or hatred. Malice, hatred and stubbornness melt away in the presence of this love. If a person desires Jesus, he will possess Him, because the Lord will, at some point in the life of each man, put him in the presence of this love. There are some who do not desire Jesus and this cannot be ignored. However, I think that in the core of most men there is a desire for safety and love.

In the place of the divine will, there are choices to be made and struggles to be overcome. The man is changing in this place and this is good. If the man stops struggling, he risks being drawn out and back into the world, where it is not spiritually safe. We must not be complacent, but if we rely on the graces in the sacraments, we will have what we need to remain anchored. Once we die in our bodies, the struggle ends. If we die in the place of the divine will, it is better than if we die somewhere else, because the journey is far easier and shorter from here than from somewhere else.

With regard to sin in this place, clearly a man is capable of sin during his life even if he never leaves the place of the divine will. This must be faced squarely lest one think that because one is not telling lies or stealing, one is worthy of canonization. A priest recently expressed concern about the inability of many to identify sin. He said that people come in after long periods without Confession and say, "Bless me, Father, for I have sinned. It has been six months since my last Confession. I haven't committed any sins."

My friends, this person has very low standards indeed if he thinks he has spent six blameless months. Perhaps what he should say is, "I really haven't examined my conscience" or possibly "I'm not sure where I am getting it wrong".

I think that the sins of people in the place of the divine will might be looked at as failures in these seven characteristics of the Father. If we commit serious sin willfully, we clearly have left the place of the divine will. If we are trying to make an accurate Confession, perhaps we can look at these characteristics and see where we have not reached the mark. Periodically, we should all do a structured and detailed examination of conscience.

My fellow apostles, I state again that we must treat ourselves with the Lord's own patience and mercy. This patience and mercy should spring spontaneously from these characteristics and the company we are keeping, meaning the Lord's. However, if one finds that one is being over-scrupulous with oneself and one is feeling that one never hits the mark and that holiness is not possible, perhaps one is being tempted by the devil to self-condemnation.

It is the devil's distortions that bring a sense of self-condemnation, so I would advise an apostle who is feeling perpetually discouraged and continually saddened by his lack of holiness to lighten up and rejoice in God's mercy instead of becoming heavily weighted by his own sinfulness and the sinfulness of others. Being too scrupulous is a snare and it annoys everyone.

Right after this comes the enemy saying, "See. You are a terrible burden to others." My friends, it is for this reason why we should always be sure we are listening to Jesus and not His enemy because the enemy does not stop at little temptations and disturbances. The enemy of peace always leads us to greater and greater upset and distortion just as the King of Peace leads to greater and greater holiness and tranquillity.

How I love the image of the Good Shepherd. It speaks to me daily. In light of the Lord's illumination of the place of the divine will, I understand so beautifully why Jesus would leave the ninety-nine to go after the one. The ninety-nine are perfectly safe. They are in His Sacred Heart. No action is necessary for the ninety-nine. Of course He goes off in search of the lost ones. Given that we love Jesus so much and we understand how pained He is at the anguish of our wandering brothers and sisters, we want to be those who cause Him no worry at all. If we stay in the place of the divine will and work hard, the Lord can relax where we are concerned, leaving us to make the most wonderful progress and leaving Him free to use our prayerful compliance to obtain the graces necessary to save others.

September 26, 2007

Today I saw a woman standing at the top of the mountain. She is a religious sister serving today in the world. I saw her in the place of the divine will. Great holiness emanated from her. She surveyed the world in silence for a long time. I watched her as she took in everything. She had God's clarity and understood the meaning of all she observed. If I had to choose two words that characterized her, I would choose wisdom and silence.

Jesus wants us to emulate her.

This woman is not in denial. Neither is she excitable. She will not be lured by the enemy's attempts to draw her into spiritual disarray. She takes all that she witnesses in the world and retreats into her interior life. We would not find this woman involved in long debates about good or evil. She simply understands that she is called to become even holier in order to offset the evil of the times.

I was blessed to understand what she understood and it was clear to me that Jesus desires personal transformation to be our highest priority.

I say that she retreated into her interior life. Do I mean that she abandoned her duties in the world to do so? No. She did not. But she completed her duties with a constantly renewed awareness of her role in the mystical reality that is the battle of good and evil.

This woman advanced into the contemplative reality, meaning, she spent her time serving on the inside and the outside simultaneously. Her awareness of God's presence was constantly renewed through silence. Active participation in the contemplative reality is achievable for each of us if we observe a fixed period of silence each day. Without this silence, we cannot absorb the invisible realities of each day. Without this silence, we are prone to being drawn out of the contemplative life.

I, myself, was very awed by this woman. Her dignity alone was worth long study. I, myself, am tempted out of the contemplative reality all the time. I forget that it is a battle and object to the tediousness of the service. I know that existing in the contemplative reality is our goal. Again, we must have goals so it is best to set them. At least if we have them we know where we need to aim.

Next, Jesus took me back into the place of the divine will

and I watched serving souls for a period of time.

My gaze then shifted down to the group of souls who serve Satan. I saw their hatred for the safe ones. I watched as the devil repeatedly stirred his servants up to anger and bitterness. If those being used by Satan saw what puppets they were and how shamelessly they were being used, perhaps their pride would prompt them to convert, but of course their pride is what is being used to control them in the first place. If only one could hold a big mirror in front of them so that they could see the enemy's reflection as he mocked them. One would say, "Look. He is laughing at you. The ongoing pain in your life is a result of your sin. You are simply a sport for the enemy. He does not love you. He despises you. You are like his trained pit bulls, fashioned to attack others while Satan exults in your gullibility."

Jesus would say that He, Jesus Christ, is the mirror that reflects this truth but the ones who serve the devil turn away from Jesus. At any rate, coming back to the original point, the ones who serve the enemy hate the safe ones and seek constantly to claw out at them and draw them down into their midst. They gather near to the place of the divine will, jeering and seducing. They treat the safe ones as one would expect in the hope that the safe ones will then be tempted to respond in kind and leave the place of the divine will. This reminds me of the justifications that occur when someone is victimized or hurt and uses this as an excuse to then behave badly. He has been drawn away and must then look at the mirror of truth that is Jesus Christ and examine his behavior, repenting and then returning to the place of the divine will.

The more I look at these realities which are invisible to the human eye, the more I thank God for the great blessing that is Confession. God knew exactly what we would need to successfully complete our time on earth. The graces available in the Sacrament of Penance are a wonder to behold. If I were to summarize these graces in one word, I would use the all-important word, clarity. Through Confession, God sends clarity. This is good and necessary if one is to advance at the desired speed.

To return to a point that is important to our Father in heaven, I address again the mystical and contemplative realities.

The mystical reality is the truth that good and evil are co-existing on earth and that a spiritual war is always taking place. At any given time, there is a state of the world in terms of spiritual warfare. A person who understands this truth will be poignantly alert to God's goals with regard to brothers and sisters who are not safe. Why do I use the word poignantly? Because God cares so much for each one who is at risk. Our pain is His pain and since He loves us and we love Him, His pain must be our pain.

What will this person do, given her attentiveness? She will be vigilant in the pursuit of personal holiness so that the enemy cannot turn her into a weapon to use against God's children, regardless of their condition or disposition. In other words, the war is against the enemy, not the people the enemy is using.

It is my opinion that the enemy wants to draw us into conflict with each other and even though a person might be actively serving the enemy, it is not our business to do battle with him. Rather it is our business to do battle with ourselves, leaving Jesus Christ to do battle with the enemy, thus claiming or seeking to claim the soul. In terms of our brothers and sisters, meaning everyone in the world with us, no sins or behaviors, regardless of how bad, change this fact. If they are on earth, we must seek to bring them to the light through prayer and example and evangelization when possible and appropriate.

I am in no way denying the call to protect and defend God's truth in whatever way God asks us to do so. I am attempting to help us identify the real enemy. We understand that at death, some people choose hell. There is nothing else to say about that as it has been dealt with elsewhere. In heaven we will have no enemies.

The mystical reality is the battle between good and evil, our King and His enemy.

The contemplative reality is a concept that is very pleasing to our beloved Father. Why? He is always present with us and He ardently desires us to be always present with Him.

I understand the smallest bit of the Father's love for us. I know He loves us in all of our sinfulness and mistakes. The fact that He sent Jesus, all by itself, testifies to His good will in our regard. He wants us to do well. He hopes that we will do well. He sees any goodness in us, any attempt at holiness and He applauds this and rejoices in it. Our Father loves us.

Recently, I had an emergency intention. I knew that someone badly needed help and I knew that this person needed the help immediately and miraculously. I began to pray. I went right to the Father and mystically wrapped my arms around his neck, whispering this intention straight into His ear. I knew that if I explained it to Him, He would not deny my friend the emergency assistance he needed. I begged Him. I really did. I did so with the greatest awareness that our Father would understand me and grasp the great need. I knew that He would not fail me if I whispered it directly to Him. I trust Him because my experience of Him is that He is extremely gentle. I know He loves us. I knew that if our beloved Father knew how important this was to me, He would help. I am certain that He did. I also knew that this was so important that I had to impose on the Father's love for me. I had to borrow on His good manners, so to speak. You see, I knew that if I approached the Father in perfect trust and love, He would be unlikely to refuse me. So that is what I did. It does not hurt the cause that the Father loves this man far more than I can love him. I borrowed on that, too. I used it all.

The contemplative reality is the truth that we serve in our humanity surrounded by heaven. We are not separated from God and God is not separated from us unless we reject Him. Even if we reject Him through grave sin, He is with us, albeit not welcome in our soul, but nearby, waiting for repentance.

We are called to serve on the outside at the same time as we are resting in God on the inside and in this way all of our service is extending the divine will further. At times, we may be with another person and at the same time we are aware of the Father and His love for the person. We are alert to the Father's needs for this person and our possible role in the Father's plan for this person. Little interactions between people can do many things, given the power of the Holy Spirit. We complete our work, aware of the saints and the way in which they completed their work. We understand that the Lord has a goal for us in each moment and that His goals for our work may be invisible to us. We rest in heaven even while we serve on earth.

Such strength is drawn down into our service, my friends, and such clarity of action. This contemplative reality is truly and simply Jesus Christ working through us in every moment of our day. Silence will teach us about this truth.

September 27, 2007

Today I saw two things. I saw what a soul looked like who spent most or all of his time in the place of the divine will. His gaze remained connected to that of the Trinity. I am speaking now of the ongoing daily experience of his soul as opposed to his humanity. This man is not aware of his condition on a conscious level. He just knows he is committed to God's will in his life. From the heavenly view this looks like a man who seldom averts his eyes from the Father. It is very beautiful. God can count on him.

Next I became more aware of his humanity. He served in relative freedom from the opinions of others in that the good or bad opinions did not impact his service. This man knows that God is his judge and he experiences a form of liberation from the opinions of other people. He is free to serve God without barriers, notwithstanding the necessary struggles for holiness.

I understood many things from this vision. First of all, I can see that those who spend most of their time in the divine will possess something that we can think of as spiritual autonomy. Their relationship with the Trinity is developed to a point that they walk through life free to love others without judgment. They truly accept themselves because they view themselves through the eyes of the Savior and understand that they are doing their best. They possess what we can think of as the personal truth of the Holy Spirit.

Between Jesus Christ and each person is a truth that encompasses the whole person and the whole Trinity. The truth about the condition of each soul must be unique as each person is unique. When one becomes connected to this truth, one views with clarity the areas in himself that are pleasing to God and not pleasing to God. One then sets about making adjustments and corrections. One experiences the love of the Father and one then begins to return that love. When one enters into this reciprocal love relationship with God, one then becomes able to extend this love to others in freedom. One learns, through this reciprocal relationship, how to love others without condition.

My friends, this is so important. We say so often that we must learn to accept ourselves. We understand that the primary work in purgatory is to learn to accept our failures and the damage that we allowed to occur through our sins, along with the gap between how we lived and how Christ lived. We understand that God wants us to do this work here and be then brought straight to heaven. Today's vision has expanded my understanding of *why* God desires us to accept ourselves here.

If we enter into this reciprocal love relationship, we become vessels of divine love on earth. We can look into the eyes of another person and smile in freedom. We neither require their acceptance nor fear their rejection. We are free to love them without limit. We are freed by the light of our own personal truth.

I will make a final attempt to be clear, as this is the reason for this whole mission.

This gaze between the Creator and the created ultimately transports the person into the contemplative reality, from where the love of the Trinity pours into the world. If a person understands that God loves him and accepts him, he is at peace. As one advances into this truth, God sheds more light on the soul and the person becomes increasingly more aware of faults and temptations. Because a person is involved in this reciprocal love relationship, he has no fear of condemnation. He knows he is loved. He knows he is cherished. He knows he fits in with heaven so he has no driving hunger to fit in on earth. Therefore his holiness work is done in hope and rejoicing. Others make judgments against the person but the person is immune to the judgments of others because he is assured of salvation from the only One who matters. Because the person accepts that God is the only One who matters, that person can love even his enemies. Who cares what the world thinks of him when God has embraced him so completely?

A Chinese priest spoke recently about being imprisoned. He was joyful and calm. He said, "If we possess God in our souls, we are free. Nobody can take Him away from us, even if they imprison us."

Human love, even at its best, contains conditions and fail-safe lines. By this I mean that we love to a point. Our point may be different for each person and we will extend our fail-safe lines for our children and spouses and siblings and parents, but there is still, in humanity, a limit to how much we love.

Often, too, with humanity, our love is conditional upon receiving love from others. In other words, if someone gives love to me, I will return that love. So love is almost something that we purchase from others. I loved you, now I have an expectation of love in return.

I am describing the limitations of love that is not ignited by the Divine Lover.

I saw people in the divine will and they loved with God in freedom. They had no desire or inclination to judge others, and this is another important part. If we are connected to the truth, that is, the reality of our condition in the light of God's love, we will understand that each person must also be connected to the truth, that is, their condition in the light of God's love. Nobody, I repeat, nobody, can completely understand God's truth about another because only God has the complete knowledge of each person.

In view of this fact, it becomes ridiculous to think we can make a judgment against another. We may be fully aware of the sins of others, just as they may be fully aware of our sins, but to think that we can make a decision about their holiness or lack of holiness is really absurd. In the light of God's truth, each person will come to know where he is at fault as well as understand the degree to which he is at fault.

If we are spending any time at all making judgments against another or weighing the sins of another against our own, we are simply wasting time and allowing ourselves to be distracted from the condition of our own soul by attempting to nose into the condition of another person's soul. This is like a voyeur looking through someone's window and complaining about what he sees. If we stop staring, we will not be so offended.

Clearly, my dear friends, I am trying to encourage all of us to concentrate on God's love for us and the holiness that we return to Him.

The contemplative reality, then, must include the reciprocal love relationship between God and each man, from where His Kingdom comes.

September 28, 2007

Jesus showed me the woman again. He asked me to study her again. I did and saw the same wisdom and understanding in her eyes as she contemplated the mystical reality, that is, the struggle between good and evil in the world.

Jesus asked me to tell Him what she did. I saw her again retreating into the contemplative reality.

Jesus asked me if she understood the mystical reality, in other words, if she could see what was happening in the world. I looked through her eyes and saw clearly the people of God who were confused, wandering, committing sins with little understanding of the separation between themselves and God. I saw these things and I answered the Lord. "Yes," I said, "she understands."

"Is she despairing, Anne? Is she downhearted?

What does she talk about? Describe her countenance."

Well, the answer was no. She was not downhearted. She was full of hope. She talked about God's mercy and God's plan. She talked about salvation and the certainty of heaven. Her countenance was one of intelligent acceptance of the mystical reality, along with trust in God and His plan for this time. Jesus was helping me to see the contrast between those who study the darkness and those who study the light. This woman holds heaven's calm in her soul and she brings heaven's calm wherever she goes. She understands the truth about the character of God and this truth assures her that the world will come right.

I believe that we must be alert to the mystical reality of the war between good and evil, but we must resist the temptation to spend time in the enemy's camp. This is yet another glance at the devil being the size of a fire ant and God being the size of the Empire State Building in terms of power. This is another smack also at superiority because this woman is humble. I have seen those who talk about the darkness excessively and I say with great sadness that they do not appear to me to possess the same humility as this woman. Those who study the darkness more than the light seem to be prone to absorbing some of its characteristics.

If someone has seen evil and wants to communicate it so that others understand, and if their motive is pure, they will talk about it in a manner that is informative, warning, loving, and genuinely eager to enlighten those to whom one speaks. If someone has been negatively affected by the evil they have observed, they tend to speak like the enemy, with a certain amount of 'you fools' entering into their dialogue. And they don't want to dialogue; they want to impress upon others that they are more in the know. Well, really, what should impress us is a treatment of evil that is balanced and honest but finite, like the enemy's power.

A term that might be used to examine this idea further is 'going native' which refers to the phenomenon of missionaries becoming like those they seek to convert, as opposed to their intended goal, which is to convert the natives in their given missionary field. This is a sly process that makes one feel that he is smarter than his fellow apostles and that he understands the extent of evil more than the next apostle. It fuels superiority. We must all take heed here. God sends an enhanced understanding of evil to those whom He wishes to combat it directly, as in exorcists. Most apostles are called to simply co-exist with evil while constantly promoting what is good, that is, God. So we identify the enemy and his tactics but we do not talk about him or inflate his power to others. If we do this, we frighten others unnecessarily.

Another way to say this is as follows. We should never run out of things to say about God's mercy and love. Eternity is just about the right amount of time to fully examine God's goodness and power. Conversely, the enemy's power is limited. I believe we will, at the moment of truth, our death, come to the full understanding of evil and that will be all the study that is required.

Look at a drop of water and compare it to all the oceans in the world and that is the beginning of the difference between the enemy's power and God's power.

Do not spend time on the drop when you are called to master the oceans.

I know a very holy priest. His humility is delightful to me. His eagerness to serve God is also delightful to me. One day I saw him walking at a distance and I was struck by the way heaven seemed to emanate from him. I saw him later that day and he was very moved. He tried to articulate his feelings about God to me across a language barrier and this is how it came out.

He said, "I came here to Knock with a heavy heart because I know God's goodness but I cannot grasp it. I felt sad about my limitation in this matter. For me, it is like trying to drink the ocean. I prayed to Our Lady here. This is what happened. She made me able to drink the whole ocean. She made my soul big enough. I know now that heaven can give us the greatest understandings in an instant."

This man is a studier of the ocean, you see. He desired the truth and he desired the truth about God, not God's enemy. He was rewarded. I could see, even from a distance, that he had been wonderfully blessed.

Evil is limited. Goodness has no limits.

October 2, 2007

Today Jesus brought me up the mountain and into the place of the divine will. We continued on, back in, deeper toward heaven. We came to the place of purgation, purgatory, and the Lord allowed me to go in. I kept moving, high above the land, so great was my joy to be back in that land of honesty. I know I am safe here.

Now it is true that there is great suffering there and I had an immediate sense of the searing pain of remorse, but if I may make a comparison, it was like going into the hospital where people are suffering terribly but well cared for and with perfect assurance of complete recovery. It is not tragic or despairing but filled with hope. Today I was able to understand a distinction in the type of soul that is there.

It seems to me that there are souls there without bodies, in other words, after their deaths, and there are souls there mystically, meaning, they are still serving on earth in their life, but they are in this place mystically, in their soul. I understood in a greater way how people can and should do their purgation work during their lifetime, and, indeed, I sensed people there mystically.

To clarify, if that is possible, we know that Jesus wants us all to die and come straight to heaven. That is God's desire for us. I understood that people truly advancing in the divine will spend time in the light of this honesty, examining their sins, as well as their failures in loving God and those around them. This work is painful and introspective, done in silence and isolation, in other words, in prayer, and has the same end result that the souls in purgatory experience, that is, complete acceptance of self and others, along with little interest in the sins of others, except for examining the level to which their own failures contributed to the pain and consequent sin of those whom their actions affected.

I have a great understanding of how we are joined to heaven through the Sacred Heart of Jesus. We are truly welcomed into the place of the divine will, and we are encouraged to proceed to a point where we serve in tandem with those in heaven who have gone before us through death. The souls still alive were doing the same work. However, they were not experiencing purgatory as a physical place, with their physical senses. They were experiencing purgatory mystically within their souls.

Given this experience, I wonder how many of us complete this work during our life. I wonder if we are with the program at all. Perhaps in times past the need to do this work here was a given. There was not the great rebellion, denial and misunderstanding of these truths. I wonder if Jesus is allowing us this knowledge and extended glimpse so that we can get back with the program. With my whole heart, I believe that people will choose this when they are given the truth.

A word about how we do this is as follows. I think we must ask Jesus in silence where He thinks we are getting it wrong. Some of us will give our sins a glance but nothing deeper.

It is like cleaning a tiled floor and only picking up the big pieces of debris. One could take only a minute or two picking up the obvious pieces of rubbish and then proudly display what a person wants to think is a clean floor. At worst, one can point constantly to the lack of large debris on his own floor as evidence of his superiority over others.

At the same time, this person could be ignoring a veritable layer of dirt and dust that is finer and less obvious to the naked eye. What one wants to do is get a really good broom and sweep thoroughly, meaning, in the corners, behind the doors, and under any rugs. It is also true that by the time one has finished at one end of the floor, it is time to begin again at the other end.

This sweeping is an ongoing necessity if one is to keep the floor really clean.

The floor is our soul, the broom is our silent time spent examining our consciences and the dirt is our sin. The big debris would be the obvious sins, the finer dirt and grime is the less obvious but, frankly, more damaging to others which include failures in the seven characteristics that we are called to advance in when working in the place of the divine will. We recall the seven characteristics are gentleness, kindness, generosity of heart, truthfulness, eagerness to serve, prudence, humility.

When we see someone with these characteristics, we will know we are dealing with a holy soul.

Sometimes the Lord will allow a soul to struggle with a big piece of debris, meaning a rather obvious sin, as a thorn in his side. This helps with humility and should not, I repeat, should not stop the person from working on everything else.

A soul could become nearly a saint, even while struggling with a big piece of debris, which the Lord can lift when He chooses. The important thing is that the soul not give up working to obtain the holy characteristics simply because he is having difficulty shifting this piece of debris. I think of addiction as an example.

I would hate to think of a soul wasting this time which has been given to him by thinking, 'I will work on holiness after I quit this addiction or overcome this obvious sin.' That is a bad attitude. If the soul proceeds in holiness work, despite the obvious struggle, meaning the thorn, that soul will find that the sin eventually becomes easily overcome.

We all know holy souls who have some thorn in their sides and frankly, they make better company than those who have no obvious thorn but thin layers of dust that they think nobody can see.

I am thinking of the woman in purgatory who had a nicotine addiction but who worked constantly for the Lord. She trusted Jesus and, as such, He repaid her generously. He said, ***"My heart has no armor against a soul such as this."***

I am not advocating addiction or any other sin. I think we should work as hard as we can to eradicate all sin and acquire every possible virtue. I am simply drawing distinctions so that we will not get tricked into thinking we are either better or worse than we are.

There is no reason not to work on holiness now.

Part Three

God is Love

Intimacy

I believe intimacy is when two souls meet to the accompaniment of a special grace. This only takes place in the Lord's will. Grace creates an opening, an opportunity, and a pure exchange takes place. This can happen through words, a steady gaze, a momentary glance, or a physical touch. We know this is happening when something goes and something comes back and both are changed, altered in some way.

Here is one example of what intimacy is not.

There are times when, through proximity, we are allowed what I will call glimpses of knowing about someone. Families are the easiest place to identify this phenomenon. These moments are moments when we have light regarding another's interior condition, his pain, his vulnerabilities, his weaknesses. Usually in families and usually amongst people of good will, these glimpses of knowing create greater compassion and respect for others. In people of bad will, these glimpses will be exploited to gain power over another. It should be noted that amongst people of good will, there is emotional safety and amongst people of bad will, there is emotional danger.

The greater the goodness in people, then, generally speaking, the greater the emotional safety.

These glimpses of knowing are precious and should be protected and respected.

I draw a distinction between moments of intimacy and glimpses of knowing in order to elevate intimacy to its proper level because it is possible that a person will experience only a handful of such moments in his life.

Now the intimacy between God and man, the Savior and the saved, happens in prayer or in special moments of grace when perhaps for an instant one senses God's presence and one knows he is loved. In these moments, two beings are open, God and the person. An exchange takes place. Something goes out and returns, in grace that unites and confirms, alters and blesses. Both the Creator and the created feel joy. Great courage comes to the created one in this exchange.

With regard to intimacy between people, this exchange can be allowed by heaven for many reasons:

To encourage each other in God's will.

To decrease the isolation of serving in exile.

To both teach and learn about pure heavenly love.

To confirm a heavenly ordained bond so that God can be glorified between two people by His plan for their joint service.

In heaven, everyone is open to both giving and receiving God's pure love. It is for this reason there are no barriers in heaven.

This pure intimacy is perfectly in tune with the timelessness of heaven so it is not lost when one person dies or both die. It will always exist. It exists in the divine will which is the heavenly Kingdom, so it never passes away. Rather, when both people arrive in heaven, the intimacy between them continues and naturally advances.

There are no limitations to this love and consequent intimacy. On earth, this can take place between two children, a man and a woman, two men, two women, a parent and a child, two siblings or a husband and wife. Intimacy is in no way limited.

In this way, we understand that there can be a marriage with no intimacy because of a lack of openness to God's grace.

Saints experience this giving and loving constantly in heaven and people experience it steadily on earth as they increase in holiness. Such joy is available to God's children. Because this experience is so special, it stands out. Many recall these moments, even if they do not understand exactly what took place. These moments can come at times of great suffering, great joy, at moments of sorrow, or simply moments of quiet. Intimacy usually sneaks up on two people when they least expect it, startling both with its intensity.

Now a husband and wife in a sacramental union are intended to share moments of intimacy such as this. The grace will be available to them but it must be accepted by both people and then shared. It is a flowing out of this grace that can take place during the physical expression of sexuality in a marriage, but it is not a given that such a flowing out takes place as many are open to the physical expression of sexuality but not open to the emotional and spiritual expression of love in their sexuality.

To depart from marriage, we must deal with the situation where God wills and then allows intimacy between a man and a woman who are not husband and wife. There clearly should be no physical expression of sexuality between them. This is a given, of course, but it must be stated, particularly at this time in history as it seems that we are able to talk ourselves into just about anything. Any sexual expression between the two people not in a sacramental union must be considered as a misfire, a mistake which takes away from the heavenly goals of the intimacy as opposed to taking the two further into the goals of the intimacy.

Both parties in this situation know this instinctively. Sexual actions outside of God's will can only damage intimacy. We see this in worldly relationships. Premature sexual sharing endangers relationships as opposed to strengthening them and this is a misuse and abuse of God's treasure.

Intimacy is a foretaste of heaven and moments when pure

love is exchanged in intimacy are timeless and ageless. These moments are preserved, never to be lost. In heaven, we will begin with these moments with each other and proceed deeper into them as well as proceeding in pure love and intimacy with others. All relationships in heaven are this way, that is, they are perfectly intimate because each soul is united to Christ so it is Christ united with a soul that loves Christ united to another soul. This is possible here on earth. The greater our unity with Christ, the greater our capacity to recognize and love Christ in others.

When loved ones die and go before us, they do not experience this as a separation because on separating from their bodies, they enter into truth and the truth is that there are no separations, no time. All is present and our loved ones see that those moments of true intimacy have remained, to be instantly reclaimed upon reunion.

So many people, when grieving their lost loved ones say, "I wish my loved one knew how much I loved him or how much he hurt me, or how sorry I am that I hurt him or how grateful I am to him or how grateful he should be to me." This is painful and unnecessary because once our loved ones die, they do know these things. They know exactly where they failed in love and exactly where they succeeded in love.

The Creator created each one of us with such love and such tenderness. The bond between God and each one of us is there, even when it is not honored by us in our humanity. The Father's total devotion to each one of us is actively expressed in the presence of Jesus Christ.

Jesus Christ crucified in the timelessness or the eternal present that is truth, longs for comfort from each one of us personally. The hunger of the Lover for the beloved can only be satisfied by one person, that is, the beloved. It is not possible for any one or any thing to provide the consolation that can quench the thirst poor Jesus crucified feels for each one of us. God, in His pure love, desires a love response from each of us in this way.

Imagine the Lord's painful longing on the cross. Because of this true bond of intimacy, between the Creator and the created, God is vulnerable to being wounded in the person of Jesus Christ. The longing He feels for each one of us insures that He feels a painful craving for, as an example, my love. My love and devotion will satisfy His longing for me, but it will not satisfy His hunger for the reader's love.

I am saying that our devotion to Him will console Him in His pain, but nothing can replace His ache for each individual and this is why the vertical relationship between Jesus Christ and each person is irreplaceable and unrepeatable.

Once I prayed to St. Therese and told her that I loved her. She began to speak and said, *"I love you, too, Anne, and we are all linked together because the love of God is such a force that it fills us all in heaven and flows out through us and between us and through us also to each person on earth. Our brothers and sisters on earth, meaning the Church militant, experience the same thing, albeit imperfectly because of their remaining humanity, but it is God's love and the reciprocal response of love for God which bonds us together."*

Yes, only the beloved can ease the terrible ache and pain Jesus feels. Even the smallest glance of love from us, the Lord's beloved, can provide relief, joy and intimacy for Him. We must never underestimate our power to console and comfort the Divine Victim. Once the Lover claims the heart of His beloved, meaning each one of us, He can rest in the commitment of His beloved and in that relative security He can then see about other affairs through us and together with us, proceeding, as it were, from the solid foundation that is the bond. The two, Jesus and the individual, proceed as one.

We must desire to be this for Jesus, to be possessed by Him and then used by Him to promote the interests of our larger family. Our apostolic commitment to Jesus should secure reliability for Him. This will happen if we work constantly to both always become and always remain a suitable host to His presence.

We want to be everything we can for Him, understanding that the Lord craves love from each member of humanity. To satisfy Him, something that becomes our heart's greatest desire, we seek to obtain for Him all that His heart desires and that includes each of our brothers and sisters. This, my friends, is why we work to bring souls to Jesus. Our love for Him and our love for them, our brothers and sisters, prompts us always to seek reunion between each of them and Jesus Christ. Our love for each of our brothers and sisters is part of the pure love that flows out from the Father and is returned by us.

When we love someone with pure love, we want them to experience joy and safety and peace and security. We want them to know they are loved and to possess this love in their heart. There is no greater joy for one who loves than to see the object of his love happy and secure, at peace with themself. The true lover desires this so much that he becomes selfless in his love. He becomes disinterested in even staking a claim on the happiness possessed by the beloved. I am reminded of St. Therese saying that she did not care if Jesus knew that the sacrifices that consoled Him came from her. This stated, the purity of love is such that it insures a connection between the two.

I can see a woman, formerly a fallen-away, sitting in prayer and I can rejoice, brought to tears because of the joy I know the Lord feels at her beautifully disposed soul. I have nothing to do with this. What is between her and Jesus is intimate and irreplaceable and completely separate from me and yet I can rejoice perfectly because I know it makes Jesus happy.

Does the Lord's love for her in any way take away from His love for me or from His joy in our relationship? No. On the contrary, it is the intimacy between us that makes me know His joy and when I turn from the consideration of this scene, He is still completely present in me.

I am female and Jesus is male so I can easily revel in the description of the relationship as the Lover and the beloved because the genders work in a way similar to that of human lovers. To examine the feelings of men with Christ I can examine my relationship with Mary, our Mother.

I feel for Mary very strongly. There is a similar intimacy in that the Father's love flows powerfully through her. She does not possess me in the same way that the Lord seeks to possess me but I do feel a total connection to her will, which always reflects the will of the Father. I feel the same sensitivity to her pain, her desires, her determination to see her Son glorified and all of her children safe and loved and connected. I want these things for Our Lady, just as I want Jesus to have the love He so craves from each of the Father's children.

Upon examination of these relationships, the word I would use to describe them is secure. These secure love relationships allow the beloved, meaning each one of us, to proceed out and continue returning love for hostility. God is all love so He can only love, but we, as His apostles, provide for Jesus so many sources of grace obtained and drawn from our sacrifices and our efforts to align our wills to His. God draws from our holiness to convert others. It is all about love expressing itself in commitment and ongoing sacrifice to the commitment. We must be like Jesus, the Lover, who exhibits the perfect willingness to suffer for His beloved ones, even at the hands of those beloved ones.

I am saying that we must be willing to accept hurt from others in order to preserve and further the bonds and teach others about love. An apostle must try to develop the following attitude toward those around him:

I am willing to accept your imperfect version of love in order to encourage you to keep trying and to teach you about love. I am willing to return heaven's version of love, regardless of what you give to me in the way of love, so that you can see what pure love looks like. This is what Jesus does for me and as such I must become more and more willing to do this for others.

This returning of pure love for imperfect love, will, with God's grace and even the smallest measure of good will in others, gradually elevate our relationships higher and higher until our relationships begin to more closely resemble the relationships between the saints in heaven. What a wonderful goal for us all.

So then, the most important message to communicate to others is that we are willing to be patient while we each learn to love like the saints in heaven love, understanding that while the hearts of others are immeasurably lovable, these hearts are temporarily wrapped in a humanity which can, at times, interfere with their heart's pure functioning.

Yes, the heart has been created to both give and receive pure love. We are intended to inhale love from heaven and exhale love to each other. Our mystical relationships, those with Jesus, Mary, and the saints, are easy in comparison to the relationships we have with those around us. We have no trouble loving the heart of God and the hearts of the saints and those who have gone before us because their hearts are no longer wrapped in humanity. While they retain their human nature, their humanity is transfigured and free of all defects and sins.

There are two types of hurtful behavior that can come from

the struggles. One is easily forgiven and overlooked, the other more difficult. One kind of hurtful behavior comes when people are trying to protect themselves from vulnerability. This is not rooted in bad will.

The other type of hurtful behavior seeks to injure, humiliate, and destroy and is rooted in bad will. It is a distortion of love. The first is easily overlooked by one who loves because it is rooted in honesty. The second is rooted in deception.

Jesus experiences this from us but the sins we commit of the first type are easily overcome through repentance and Confession. The second type are not as easily overcome because the anti-love quality originates in a lie. "I'm not hurting you. I'm not sinning. You are the problem. Your rules and requests are unreasonable."

One draws pure love and reconciliation and the other repulses pure love because it is like an opposing magnet.

The first one is capable of hurting, yes, and wounding the heart but the first is always drawn back to reconciliation and genuinely seeks what is good for the Lover. Because of this core of goodness, the Savior always looks past the humanity and directly into the potential.

Parents get lovely glimpses in their children of the adult that is to come and Jesus sees lovely glimpses in us of the saints that we will become. Anti-love does not seek the good of another or the best interests of another. The anti-lover, Satan, seeks to exploit for his own purposes and agenda and it is this that repels.

We, God's apostles, must love each other with a pure love but even pure love does not presuppose intimacy. We cannot command intimacy with another any more than Jesus Christ can command intimacy with any one of us. Intimacy occurs when accompanied by grace, as stated. Intimacy could be thought of as being connected in grace, through grace, and I believe intimacy is an action of grace. It is a gift from heaven and can only be received through heaven's action.

All the saints in heaven are permanently connected to each other in this way and love each other in this way.

People often experience intimacy during or because of great suffering. Suffering is underrated as a life experience. I say this because we usually abhor it and yet it brings such sublime delights, one of them being an increased opportunity for intimacy with those around us.

Now, it is true, as we stated, that we cannot command intimacy with another even with pure love, but that does not mean our giving of pure love is a wasted exercise. There is no such thing. Love always benefits the lover and the beloved. Consider a family member stubborn in bitterness. Can or should the family members stop offering pure love, either through loving contact or consistent prayer when there is separation? No. We should keep praying and hoping and loving, even if we must do so from a distance.

Ultimately, this pure love will advance the Lord's interests in the person's soul, either through healing and conversion during life or conversion at the moment just before death. Truly, the non-accepting party is still the recipient, if only as one who has at the very least been given an example of the true form of love as opposed to what this world is offering in the way of love.

In many cases, one party must offer pure love consistently, without a return, and only over time will the other become willing to accept this pure love.

It should not discourage any of us that we do not always know how to love. This should not even slow us down, any more than a small child going off to school for the first time is concerned that he does not know how to read. On the contrary, our awareness of our difficulty in loving others should make us seriously determined to show up for heaven each day, presenting ourselves to Jesus Christ as willing and eager students.

Suffering with Love

Suffering pain and being tempted to bitterness ... how is it that these things proceed into compassion?

The divine pain includes a build-up of love that inflates like a stretched balloon inside our hearts. The experience of love increasing is one of near agony and the recipient feels as if he will be annihilated by the extent of the anguish from the love he feels.

One wonders, how did Jesus cope?

Now this love, as stated, seems to grow and grow through the recipient's life experiences of pain, bitterness, betrayal, and all things that are repugnant to us in our humanity. Who would choose such experiences? Who would sign up for them? Surely, only Jesus Christ and yet each of us who directs our steps after Him does so in willingness to accept at least some of His life experience.

On the outside we see suffering. Our humanity trembles with the weight of the suffering. At times, we are certain we will be overcome. But, if taken with heaven, our heart fills and fills and fills on the inside.

We must accept, believe, and trust that Jesus supports the soul as it is being filled and stretched to a seemingly unbearable limit. And then, the Lord Himself, at His pleasure and in accordance with His holy plan, opens a valve and love begins to flow out to others, on and on, further and further into the world, creating the most delightful and inexplicable divine ripple effect.

My brothers and sisters, how patiently Jesus has prepared us for love, how tirelessly and scrupulously He forms us, stretching the heart steadily in order to make it strong enough for its ultimate purpose, perpetual and complete intimacy, which is, as we said, a cloudburst of love.

Because this love is divine, it must flow along the river of the divine will. We, in our humanity, often would like to direct its flow toward those whom we think it would be humanly pleasing to love and be loved by. And yet Jesus, in His wisdom, puts His hand up, knowing that our love, divine in nature, will be like seeds among rocks, wasted and dishonored. Oh that we could follow His will from infancy, but then again, it is in the departures from His will that we experience the lovely reconciliation with all its opportunity for humility and compassion. God's plan is so vast.

Now, why does Jesus seem to require such searing suffering in order for us to be filled with this love? I am not sure, but I know that suffering produces compassion. Our willingness to accept suffering and humiliation for love of Christ, our refusal to turn our backs to Him or turn our gaze away from Him is what insures that this balloon will be filled. Temptation comes with suffering and persecution, it is true, but we will resist temptation with God's grace. And His compassion for the suffering of others will fill us.

Who loves like the Trinity, humanly present in the Lord's humanity? Nobody. Jesus, in not only His Passion and death but in His life, experienced a constant, steady, relentless filling of His human heart with divine love. Surely the divine pain Jesus felt must have been nearly unendurable. I believe that in some ways the Passion might have provided mystical relief, a final outpouring of love so unlimited that it became a roaring river that never diminishes.

In our own experience, we will find that the Lord opens the valve to release this love that He has packed into us, when He needs to, and therefore, because it is His, we must be willing to love whomever Jesus wants to love through us at His every whim.

Jesus, the Lover, always alert, watches His beloved. If the

beloved shows signs of weariness or discouragement, the Lover moves swiftly to refresh and encourage.

There are times when the beloved, that is, each one of us present in this distinct and separate relationship with Christ, rejects assistance. We have all had the experience of someone whom we may characterize as difficult to love. Often by this we mean that someone does not find it easy to accept our love, perhaps because of a feeling that he is unlovable. There will always be those in our lives who give us the feeling that we are trying to love a cactus plant. If we get too close, we get hurt. Jesus experiences this, too, of course, with each one of us to different degrees at different times in our lives.

The Lover, Jesus Christ, feels the pain of His beloved acutely, suffering with us the pains of our humanity. How baffling for Him, humanly speaking, to be rejected, and yet how patiently He awaits acceptance. His whole presence in each relationship could be viewed, among many other things, as a study in patience. We, the beloved ones, entertain so rarely the truth of the constant gaze of love that follows our every breath. This is perhaps a blessing because when the strength of the Lover's gaze is remotely understood, the beloved one can feel helplessly inadequate in the love equation. How can one return such pure love? How can one measure up, protecting the pristine nature of the exchange? Clearly, without grace, one would simply drift away, such would be the hopelessness of the situation.

To protect the relationship, Christ infuses into His beloved puffs of pure love through an action of the Holy Spirit. There is no limit to the amount of growth possible in love, even while we remain on earth.

The beloved becomes more and more disposed to the Lover and gradually, in the same way, learns to become more and more alert to the Lover's whims and communications. This is to be desired, because, even while this disposition increases the divine pain of separation, it increases the capacity for storing the treasures that come from the Lover's heart.

We must all strive to be first, recipients and then storehouses of the Lover's gifts. When others see the salutary effects of these gifts, they will also seek the Lover. This love must be accepted and stored for the benefit of this recipient, the beloved one, but also for the benefit of all those around the beloved, such are the magnificent emanations from pure love.

The Lover is always fully engaged with us. That does not and will not change. The process we desire or strive for is to enter into the gaze, to become fully engaged with Him in a constant exchange.

Distractions fade as one progresses because the walls of the gaze become more pronounced and more adept at repelling those things that seek to tear the beloved away from the process.

An action of grace from the Trinity preserves the recipient of the Savior's love.

Craving love from each other is a good thing. This makes us like Christ who craves our love. Yet, in this time, many feel ashamed that they crave love from others. The greater the love we feel for others, the greater the craving for a reciprocal response of love. Our craving does not insure that we will receive that which we crave, any more than the Lord's craving for love from each man is satisfied.

Happily, Jesus teaches us as much in rejection as He teaches us in acceptance, that is, the experience of rejection, being so consistent with the ongoing experience of Jesus Christ by humanity, enables us to further identify with the crucified Christ.

When the Lord suffered Calvary, He suffered or

experienced near-total rejection. This was His experience of it in His humanity, even though we know that not all mankind rejects Christ. Did this cause Him to return rejection or abandon His love for us? No. On the contrary, in the acceptance of those who rejected Him, Jesus set an example of heavenly and unconditional love. Jesus' acceptance of the rejection of others in no way diminished His craving for the love of humanity. He craved love in both His humanity and His divinity until the moment of His death. He continues to crave our love and safety.

The more we possess Christ, the more we recognize Christ and love Him in others.

This pain of separation then extends at times to others who also possess Christ. In other words, those who have grown to love Christ identify Him in others. They respond to His presence in others, even though they may not know what it is they are drawn to or what it is they are craving. How terribly confusing at times, but how wonderfully exciting that we can have this heavenly experience to any degree at all while remaining in our humanity. This is truly another foretaste of heaven.

Observations on Love

Where is the fail-safe line when it comes to love? At what point do we examine love and determine that it is too costly an endeavor?

In terms of humanity, the line is movable from one person to the next and from one relationship to the next. In heaven, there is no line. There is no limit to the sacrifice willingly given for others.

Where was the line for Jesus?

There was no line, of course, and that is the point of the Passion. Jesus gave and gave and gave until His body expired.

Those reading this work are not yet in heaven and as such do not have experience of this limitless love. We are compelled to love in a pitifully limited way because of the filter of our humanity and consequent self-interest. This, our limited ability to overcome self and love in purity, is coupled with the limitation of others in accepting pure love. Given these two apparent handicaps, it could be called amazing that any love be exchanged on earth at all.

And yet, just as God is present in our humanity, so is love and the potential for love present in our humanity.

I suppose that as neophytes in love, we must study the Great Lover and try to emulate Him. How does Jesus love us?

Jesus knows that we have difficulty in accepting too much love too fast. He knows that it is counterproductive to swamp us. Jesus knows that while love must be patient, it must also be constantly alert. When love is constantly alert, it will never miss an opportunity to be present when the smallest opening arises. At the appointed time, the opportunity arises, and Love, opportunistic in the extreme, flows into the beloved one.

What is the experience of this for the recipient? Well, I

think it must be useless to describe it because it is so unique to each person. However, we should at least describe the symptoms that love has been there, that love indeed happened in a place.

When we have accepted the love of Christ, even for a brief instant, we are calmed. An interior awareness of our dignity and unique value begins to grow. With the awareness of our own dignity comes a greater awareness of the dignity of others. In other words, it is only when we accept pure love from Christ that we can give pure love to others. We could observe then that those who exhibit the greatest amount of pure love for others are those who themselves have been the greatest recipients of pure love. When we accept the love of Christ, we then have something of value to offer others. Absent this divine love, we can only offer a love to those around us that is rooted in self, that is exploitative, suspicious, and cynical. It is this selfish love that seems to abound in this time and which does so much damage. People have an expectation of pure love and they do not receive it. Poor suffering humanity has little awareness of the extent or source of its pain.

If we are to learn to live like citizens of heaven, then we must learn to love.

It is true that love sometimes bubbles up delightfully and needs no instruction. New parents studying the face of their infant for the first time do not need tuition in love. A child has little difficulty loving his mother and father, his sister, his brother. We certainly begin love lessons in our immediate families. At home, in our immediate families, love is often, if not usually, reciprocated.

We are then expected, as Christians, to bring our

knowledge of love into the world. It becomes a little more difficult out in the world because love is more likely to be misunderstood or rejected. Still, our obligation remains. Jesus told us to love one another. He did not say love one another and make sure others love you back.

Let us look, initially, at two situations. One will be an example of pure love and the other will be an example of a worldly version of love, which we will look at first.

A man has suffered a terrible tragedy. This tragedy came to him suddenly and unexpectedly. He has been left shocked. His humanity reels from his attempt to take it in and accept it. He spends most of his time in silence and prefers to be alone.

A friend arrives, determined to cheer him up. The friend notes the serious and sad look on the sufferer's face and in his heart he is annoyed. He begins to talk animatedly about the world in general and people they know. The victim of the tragedy is unable to abandon his grief to enter into this chatter, although for the sake of good manners he mutters appropriate replies. His friend can see clearly that the man is not responding positively. He is not cheering him up and he knows it. How could he when this man's world has caved in? Why should the victim be cheerful?

Does the visitor change tactics? Does he abandon the expectation of normalcy and open a door to the man's grief? No. He instead stares ahead, annoyed. Then, giving a big sigh, leaves.

The visitor is irritated by the pain. He arrived with no intention of entering into the circle of anguish. He did not want to because it hurts there, where the friend is residing. His actions, while good on the surface, meaning he showed up to visit, lack pure love because in fact he is not willing to suffer with the friend. Instead he wants the friend to enter into his circle of apparent wellness. When the sufferer does not abandon his grief, because he is unable to, the friend adapts a martyred air. *I am here to cheer him up and he won't let me. He is rejecting me. He is selfish. He should get on with it.* And then, *There's nothing I can do for him so I will stay away.*

There are degrees of malice in this, of course. In some cases people are simply unable to deal with strong emotions. They are frightened by them and have not developed the capacity to accept these emotions, particularly when the emotions flood as in the case of grief. But there are other times when a person is simply indifferent, unwilling and uninterested.

Let's examine another possibility.

The same man is stuck in the same grief. His friend arrives, but prior to arriving he has given the matter some thought and prayer. He prepares himself to be available to his friend in whatever way is welcomed and needed. In other words, he relinquishes all thought of himself before he arrives. He goes with no self-interest. He goes with the understanding that he needs to enter into the grief of his friend, regardless of how painful that will be, and that he should not try to pull his friend out of the grief.

The sufferer appears despondent and is not prone to talking. The friend remains silent, accordingly, and waits. The compassion in his silence is communicated through the Holy Spirit. Words are unnecessary. One of them, either the sufferer or the friend, makes reference to the tragedy. This is a must because the tragedy is present, as surely as the chairs are present.

The friend inquires from the sufferer as to how he is coping. He is legitimately interested in the pain of the man. He is prepared to let the man talk and talk and talk if necessary. If the man chooses not to talk, the friend does not take it personally. He is not insulted because he has not gone to be affirmed but to affirm.

This is pure love. It accepts hurt through understanding.

If the sufferer does not speak, does this friend then stay away? No. He returns regularly in the same way, with no expectations from the sufferer, prepared always to remain in the grief of the wounded one. We must understand that the sufferer has been blessed by the willing companionship of his friend. He may not be able to express his gratitude because he may be too angry at the tragedy, or too stunned, but when he is able to verbalize something, the friend will be there and the friend will listen and accompany him.

I often think of St. John the apostle at the foot of the cross. We could look at St. John's role in the Passion and think correctly, 'My goodness, what a privileged position St. John was awarded.' In considering the matter, one might wonder what qualified St. John to accompany Jesus and Mary so intimately on this torturous day.

What we know about St. John is that he was remembered by the purity of his love. He is called the Lord's beloved apostle. What did love prompt him to do that day that nobody else did? He showed up, first of all, and then he stayed. The day got uglier and uglier, the crowds more venomous. It did not appear to be a day of triumph, even though we know it turned out to be so.

St. John showed up, and he stayed.

Was Jesus able to verbalize his tremendous gratitude to John at the time of His Passion? Was Jesus able to chat about John's concerns? Hardly. He had his hands full dealing with His own considerable difficulties. The best Jesus could do was to assign John a task. ***"Son, behold your mother."*** Was there any other apostle there to accept this task? No. Just John.

I would guess that John did not do a lot of talking on that day. I would guess he just stayed, suffering Jesus and Mary's anguish, uniquely willing to remain in a circle of suffering and grief that could be called unparalleled. Is there a greater example of loyalty, love or fellowship?

Can we imagine the Lord's gratitude even though it was not expressed on that day? I do not think so. I do not think we can ever imagine the extent of the Lord's gratitude to St. John. I think, though, that His gratitude resonates throughout heaven, eternally preserved.

We are called to be like John to each other. We are called to show up for each other and we are called to stay, often in silence or in service or in silent service. This is pure love.

Why does pure love seem to be so elusive during this time?

Well, we are called the Me Generation. That, all by itself, is a condemnation of our times. Love cries out for sacrifice but many of these cries go unheard. In some cases, the cries are mocked. People are encouraged to seek satisfaction for themselves. But we are a community people, intended to give and accept Christ in each other. If I am wholly concentrated on serving myself and filling my own needs, I become unavailable to serve others.

As stated, people crave love as Christ craves love. This is the way we are created. But now some people experience guilt about this as though they are not worthy of being loved or as though they are not entitled to be loved or even as though they are asking too much in expecting to be loved. There are many making do with crumbs from the table when they should be experiencing a great Christian feast.

We should never be ashamed that we crave love, from God, from each other, and from the world around us. Each person is created to be valued and loved and in this period of great advances, there is a historically unique opportunity to live out the Christian call to honor each of God's created children.

There are people who have this vision and who are trying to do this. They are feeding the hungry, comforting the poor and preaching reconciliation to warring individuals. They are spreading the Gospel message. There needs to be more of them. The number of those who act in love must increase and certainly will increase in this time of renewal.

Is it possible that people have become distracted? Or that material belongings have been used as an opiate for the masses in the affluent West? People crave material possessions. They crave material possessions as they once craved love. The need for love has been relegated to a subordinate position.

We know that when children experience a nutritional deficiency, they fail to flourish. Their little bodies stop growing at the correct speed. They develop various symptoms of the deficiency and become unwell, sometimes to small degrees and sometimes to serious and even dangerous degrees. The point is, though, that we can identify symptoms.

It is the same way in this time. We are all like children in our need for love and many of us are developing symptoms of this love deficiency. We see this in the rate of depression, anxiety, suicide, broken families, violence in children and in families. To say that it has always been this way is to speak in denial. We may not want to believe this. We may not want to correlate a decrease in faith with a decrease in wellness but the truth is the truth. When God was abandoned, the supply of love decreased.

April 4, 2008

Today the Lord showed me a young boy of about twelve years of age. The boy was home playing a game by himself. The father arrived home and I could see that the boy was very lonely for his father's company. The father was a congenial man who loved his son but he was moving fast through his life and was not interacting with the son. Yes, the son craved the father's company and the father was not at peace because he was not expressing his love for his son, meaning through his actions.

I asked Jesus to explain this. It was clear that there was ample love present but at times people appear to be locked in habits of emotional separation.

Jesus showed me that there was acrimony between the husband and wife. Because of this unresolved conflict between the couple, there was bitterness present. With bitterness, people do not feel safe or inclined to let love flow through them freely. I could see that if the situation between the couple was resolved, the wife would pass a few gentle words to the husband and he would engage with the son. It really only needed gentle reminding and suggesting as the wife was attuned to the son's craving for his father. But because of this block between the couple, anything that the wife said came out harshly. She is hurt and wants her husband to seek forgiveness. She craves unity but neither is currently able to move toward it.

Jesus then showed me that He was watching carefully and waiting for an opportunity. God wants this family inhaling heaven's love and exhaling it to each other. He wants this block healed. I understood that if one of the parents would offer a word of conciliation to the other, the Lord would absolutely incinerate any hard feelings. This couple loves each other. There is no problem there. How frustrated Jesus must become with us. I asked Him what was needed and He said, **"Humility. One of the parents must humble themselves before the other and seek peace. That is all that is required. As soon as one of the**

parents comes to Me, I will instruct them accordingly."

I felt peace in this as I know the Lord is going to fix this and this is probably the case in every marriage at some time, but the point that remained with me was that, as parents, we really have to sacrifice pride to preserve a loving exchange in our relationships. I could see clearly in this case how this child was being affected by the difficulty of the parents. We must pray for holy marriages.

Loving Those Who Have Fallen Away
from the Church

There are many Catholics who have fallen away. Now, there have always been and there will always be those who step away from their faith for a time and then return. A difficulty in this time is that the enemy has so smeared the reputation of the priesthood that people who have fallen away do not as readily identify a point of entry back into the Church. In the past, people would be aware of a priest in their life and they would go to him and they would generally be encouraged in their desire to return. The priest would usually then wade through the obstacles with the person.

How sad for Jesus. How terribly sad for those who have fallen away and ache to return. I believe that people suffer dreadfully from an emotional wedge between them and their priests. For those serving steadily in the Church, there is no such wedge, of course. God's priests serve us and we love them and thank God for them. With others away from the Church, however, there is a separation and it is almost as though they do not feel it is right to love their priests and they feel guilty for any affection they feel for them. This campaign of ugliness was planted a long time ago by Satan and it is only now that his hurtful harvest is being seen to its real extent. With God's grace it is the end of this period.

We will know when we have this situation when we hear someone talking about the one priest they know who is 'all right,' 'normal' or 'what they should all be like.' The implication, of course, is that most are not 'all right,' 'normal,' or 'what they should all be like.' This can severely try the patience of those of us who know many holy priests, but we must take it gently and understand that these individuals are looking for entry back into communion with God's priests and God's Church. It is as though the one or two priests they know and cannot help but love, somehow give them permission to once again love and honor the priesthood in general. We must be patient and assist in this process as much as possible.

There are many fallen-away Catholics who claim to reject either God or the Church or perhaps all organized religion. Close observation of these individuals will reveal many who are living out much of the Christian message, despite their claims that they do not follow Christ. How can there be such goodness, which we know always originates in God, from those who claim to reject Him?

I believe that in many cases, rejection of God or the Church is not really rejection at all. What these people are really rejecting, rightfully in some cases, is one person or a handful of persons' misrepresentation of God, the Church, or organized religion in general. They are rejecting hypocrisy. That makes them just like Jesus and just like us. If we are thinking men at all, we also reject hypocrisy. It sickens us. These people have fallen into the trap of painting all professed Christians with the same brush. They make cruel generalities, which is often the very sword that sliced into them.

A holy nun once retired. A fallen-away who knew her well said, with great feeling, "To me, she is what religion is all about. If only there were more like her." Well, I heartily agreed with him, of course, that she was what religion is all about, but the implication was that this nun was the only one of her kind or one of a few amongst many. It is back to the statement "If all priests were like him." We are back to the assumption that most religious people are hypocrites. This is fearfully limited thinking and has contributed to the misunderstanding of many.

But back to the original thought, the reason that people who espouse rejection of God can bring so much good into the world and love, even without benefit of open practice of faith, is that they have not really rejected Christ. They have just abandoned His Church. God will reward their goodness, of course, and I believe that at the time of their death Jesus will compel notice of Himself, but the situation is heart wrenching because Jesus does not deserve to be verbally rejected, even if the rejecters live out His message. He, Jesus Christ, deserves credit for the Christian message if only to reveal the truth for others.

It goes without saying that it is better to live the Christian message than to simply talk about living the Christian message. However, it also goes without saying that it is even better to both live the Christian message and proclaim the Christian message, giving credit at all times to Jesus Christ, the source of the message.

Jesus does not want His Church misjudged and slandered. He wants His Church vigorously defended. Jesus sends the greatest sacramental graces through the Church and those who have decided to do without these graces are in actual fact rejecting the very food that nourishes holiness. Also, God, as the source of all wisdom, knows the most effective ways to assist humanity. If we are serving with Him, He can direct our efforts in a way that makes them abundantly fruitful, far more fruitful than if we do not access and heed His direct counsel.

Perhaps those fallen-aways who were baptized Catholic can be encouraged to meet the Jesus of the Bible. If one studies Jesus Christ scripturally, one falls in love with Him. He was fair, just, and always loving. Since all of Christianity is based on the Lord's life, it would seem wise to have a good look at Him personally before rejecting Him and the way of life He began. While doing this, one could ask the Lord to reveal Himself if He chooses.

At that point, after one has studied Jesus in Scripture and found Him to be good, perhaps the one who searches for truth should sit with Jesus in front of the tabernacle. As Catholics, we believe in the Lord's true presence in the Eucharist, which He Himself announced on Holy Thursday at the Last Supper. The one who has rejected his faith could then ask the Lord to reveal Himself through the Eucharist.

Next, perhaps the searcher will ask the Lord to reveal His presence in the soul of another person, one who loves as Jesus loves, one who seeks Christ as the searcher seeks Christ, with an open heart and in truth. These apostles are everywhere, awaiting the inspiration of the Holy Spirit. Jesus will connect the one who seeks Him to holy fellowship when the time is right and persuade the searcher that while all Christians are human, all Christians are not hypocrites.

This strategy for truly understanding what one is rejecting, seeks Christ in three ways: in Holy Scripture, in the Eucharist and ongoing life of the Church, and in other faithful Christians.

These are good places to look for Jesus because He truly lives and ministers to us from these three places each day if we seek Him.

What is the Lord's experience of this time? I believe that the Lord sees many of His children living outside of the safety of His Church and He is sorrowful. Why is He sorrowful? Is it because Jesus wants to control people? Is it because Jesus wants to be justified and powerful? Is He concerned about His glory? Hardly. Jesus is sorrowful because He wants to provide safety for His children and He cannot protect us when we reject Him.

I believe that the Lord sees the spiritual and emotional and even physical danger of life lived in rebellion and He mourns our denial of these realities.

What will help?

Do we need more people preaching the Gospel? Yes. We do. At once. We need more truth tellers and fewer hypocritical representations of Christ.

Do we need those preaching the Gospel to be humble? Yes. We require an increase in humility and a decrease in arrogance. The fact that those living in rebellion can be aggressive and hurtful is no excuse for us to respond with aggression and hurtfulness. We are called to be different. We should be different.

Do we need greater obedience to the Magisterium of the Church? Yes. Only God knows how damaging the level of disobedience has been. Those serving in the Church who openly reject the teaching of the Church are hurting the Lord's cause terribly. We are called to put on the mind of Christ, not the mind of the world. We just cannot all be leaders. Some of us have to follow. That is the point of the whole exercise … to follow Christ as He manifests Himself through the teachings of the Church.

Do we need more prayer? Yes. This is a compelling need for every Catholic. Less talk, more listening to heaven. We need all kinds of prayer in our days. If we learn to pray, we will learn to listen to the Holy Spirit and serve as He wills, not as we will.

I believe Jesus is hurting for each soul who has fallen away from His Church. There is the greatest temptation to become angry at the behavior of some who have fallen away. Sometimes they are remarkably arrogant. One man recently said to a devout Catholic woman, "Don't you know that the

Catholic Church is the Church you come away from, not the Church you join?"

One is tempted to say, "I beg your pardon. I am a Catholic and you know it. Have you any manners at all?" Truly, apostles, one does wonder when it became acceptable to openly insult us and our faith. If we dared to openly insult the faith of another we would hear about it in a hurry. The apostles were put to death for their faith so I suppose there is huge precedent for being persecuted. But here is the difference. The apostles vigorously defended their faith. There is often deafening silence from Catholics today.

As stated, Jesus wants His Church vigorously defended. I think we had better start defending our faith, but with gentleness, humility and good manners.

Commitments of Love

Love expresses itself in many ways. One of the ways love expresses itself is through commitment. Commitment is like a flag that is dug well and truly into the ground. It goes down deeply, so deeply that winds cannot blow it out of the position where love has placed it. If this flag is dug in, at its base there is no movement. Above ground, there may be gale force winds which tear at the flag with violence. There may be hailstones and rain that pound at the flag pitilessly. There may be other flags not anchored as well which slap against the flag with the greatest force in an attempt to dislodge it.

At times, during stormy weather, it may appear that the most prudent course for the flag would be to dig itself up and go somewhere else, particularly when there is a great fog around the flag. The flag will believe it cannot be seen anyway. What is the point of a flag if it is obscured by fog? The flag will begin to question its location.

But the flag did not place itself. It allowed itself to be placed. Our love **for** Christ has drawn us into our commitments **to** Christ. He has placed us. We must trust that He will relocate us if He needs to and until then, let the winds blow, let the fog encircle us and let others slap off us. Our commitment must keep us firmly planted in our service to heaven.

We need to remind ourselves often, sometimes daily, that our feelings must not dictate our service. On any given day we will not want to serve and our commitment might seem like a prison. When this is the case, we must make a heroic decision to be joyful prisoners.

Yes, it is true that at times we feel imprisoned by our commitment. The prison walls seem dense and punishing and the space within which we live out our response to love can feel suffocating. There can be a temptation to panic.

The more trapped we feel by our commitment, the more we should be determined to fulfill its duties. If we can sustain a calm forward motion, we will defeat the enemy's attempts to distract us and disturb us. It is helpful to think in terms of today and tomorrow. A wise apostle will say, "Perhaps tomorrow the Lord will change my commitment. For today, I must continue to serve within it." In the moments of heroism, when the apostle serves in near total darkness, Heaven does the most magnificent things, even if these things are accomplished only in the soul of the apostle.

Dearest friends, sometimes we look back at the lives of the saints and we marvel at their actions of heroic service, their moments of breathtaking fortitude. Well, those moments stand out, it is true, but I am not sure those are necessarily the most heroic moments. I believe the really heroic moments for each soul are unseen by any other soul and I believe that the person living the moment often has no idea of its magnitude.

Eloquence has abandoned me and yet this must be stated clearly.

The big things can seem easy when compared to the secret and solitary battles fought against pride, discouragement and loneliness. I believe God carries us through the big things with copious amounts of grace. 'Renounce God or die' moments would at least seem clear to the apostle. It is the enemy's sneak attacks, the temptations against the daily commitments which require the true mystical sweat of labor. These are the times when, in terrible frustration and loneliness, we are tempted to quit the more difficult commitments and retreat to safer, less taxing and demanding areas of service.

Through the struggles, love remains, the immovable

persuader, which, like a stone wall at our back, bars retreat. The eyes of Christ Crucified steadily communicate the eternal call which pierces our resistance again and again. Who can turn away from Him? Who can reject Him? Who could leave the Lord to His anguish?

Apostles, we must all be like St. John standing with Our Lady at the foot of the cross. We must all stay with Him.

Commitment is an expression of love. If love is real, then commitment will be expressed joyfully. It will not be like a big bright shirt that we put on to draw attention to ourselves. *See me living my commitment? See how I suffer?* No. This is done for purposes of securing admiration and glory. Rather, we express our love through commitment in a quiet and steady way, with a light step and a cheerful countenance, so much so that none would guess that our commitment can, at times, feel like a heavy burden.

Given that we know so little about the pure love experienced as a constant state by all the residents of heaven, it is important that we identify it where we can on earth, thereby studying it and advancing into its practice. This causes a certain amount of pain, it is true, because the more we learn what it is, the more we lament about what it is not. Such pain all around us. So many broken hearts. So many of God's children thinking sadly in their souls, *'I expected more.'*

Our consolation for each of these hurt individuals comes from our certainty that they will advance to the fullest extent of love's limitlessness in heaven, receiving infinitely.

Comparing the ability to love in heaven to the ability to love on earth is like comparing the speed and efficiency of the fastest jet on earth to travelling on a tricycle. The one travelling on the tricycle will move forward if he applies himself, it is true, but he will not initially be able to advance at the speed of the jet plane. Many are not even trying. They do not even know that the tricycle can move, never mind applying themselves to the labor of learning how it works and then pedalling.

You might observe that it is pitiful to even attempt to travel like the jet plane when we are so limited by our humanity. But there is a way around this. It is called holiness. The holier one becomes, and the more a person allows Jesus Christ to possess him, the less limited in love he becomes. Jesus can truly lift the tricycle and move it as fast as the fastest plane. This happens and it is this that the Lord wills for each of us.

A cautionary note is that when one is attempting to allow the Lord to move one at this speed, meaning to love in purity as they love in heaven, one stands out amongst those who are not as involved in this process. One becomes a target, as it were, because others do not understand. Those lounging on their tricycles with their feet draped over the handlebars will usually not admire this advanced form of movement. Rather, they will disparage it, challenge it, and even attempt to destroy it. This is how we get martyrs.

Persecutions are truly a good sign that we are doing well, as long as we are humble and resigned.

Such a tall order! How many can rejoice in persecution? Those are high flyers indeed. But again, we seek out examples so that we can at least see what this level of holiness looks like.

The apostles once left prison rejoicing that they had been found worthy to be scourged for the Gospel message.

40 And they had the apostles called in, gave orders for them to be flogged, warned them not to speak in the name of Jesus and released them. 41 And so they left the presence of the Sanhedrin glad to have had the honor of suffering humiliation for the sake of the name (Acts 5).

We might be less exuberant about persecution but that only means that we are still learning. We should be at peace in this and accept that we are not perfect. This awareness helps our humility and humility signals holiness.

I am saying that if we have not yet advanced to a state where we can rejoice in persecution, we should not be discouraged. The fact that we know we should rejoice in persecution is an excellent start.

Perhaps we are squeamish about bloody martyrdom. We may not like the idea of being slandered, maligned and scourged. Maybe, for most of us, it is all we can do to live out our commitments to Christ quietly and humbly, steadily and cheerfully, in fatigue and in discouragement, with consolation and in consolation withheld. But I feel quite certain that Jesus will teach us all to love in purity, right where He has placed us.

A Witness of Love

I remember a time during one of life's tragedies when a strange woman ministered to me. I was crouched against a wall in front of a hospital, terribly frightened as a family member was near death because of a serious accident. It was dark and a woman walked by me, hurrying along. I barely noticed her. She stopped suddenly, turned back and approached me with the greatest confidence.

"What's wrong, Honey?" she asked.

Startled, I told her in a few sentences. I was not interested in conversation, to be honest, as I had been talked to death in the immediate past few days.

"Well," she said, letting her breath out in a huge sigh, "You need Jesus Christ as sure as I'm standing here. I just knew He was asking me to stop and minister to you."

With that she dropped her purse and shopping bags. Now, she was clearly not Catholic. I *am* Catholic and as a Catholic I was raised to pray quietly in form. This woman was a big woman, with a big wild hat and brightly-colored clothes. Even her bags were wildly colored. I couldn't imagine why she was dropping everything there on the street in sub-zero temperatures. She made me extremely nervous.

I remained with my back to the wall. She put her hands over my head and let heaven have it.

"Jesus Christ," said she in a strong, loud voice, "I know You're there and I know You're listening. This poor little thing is looking like she's all alone down here and I don't like it, not one little bit. I ain't going nowhere, Lord, till You give this child the grace she has a right to expect from You. You hear me, Jesus. I know You do. Look how cold she is, Lord. Look how scared she looks. She believes in You, Jesus, and she shouldn't look so cold and scared. We need help right now."

She paused in the silence. The people gathering around us were also silent. Nervous laughter spilled out of me.

"Help us, Jesus. Help us right now." She waited again. "I'm still here, Lord. I'm not leaving until You help her."

At that point, I joined her in prayer.

Suddenly, waves of grace came down on me. All my fears left as strength poured into me. The woman put her hands on my head and warmth flowed from them. I felt such love and peace. I looked up at her in surprise and her beautiful warm brown eyes looked back at me.

"He was here all the time, Honey," she said gently. "He wouldn't leave you. You just couldn't feel Him."

With that she picked up her bags and purse and left, leaving me hugely consoled. I think of her so often over the years. This woman was paying attention. She looked tired and she walked as though her feet hurt and yet she stopped and loved me, a stranger who was nothing to her. This beautiful apostle was paying attention to Jesus.

An Invitation to Love

Peter, our rock, denied Jesus three times before being charged with the beginning of the Catholic Church, a fact which assures us that our Church was built on heaven's acceptance of our humanity. One might say that our whole Church is founded upon both repentance and forgiveness. Our weaknesses are understood by heaven and must be accepted by us despite our distaste and revulsion for our sins. The apostolic tradition includes humility which comes from the constant need to accept both our own mistakes and the mistakes of others.

We are all on the same team, welcome in God's family to the same degree. Are some sinners more worthy of forgiveness than others? Are some people more welcome in the Church than others? The Ring of Defiance must be pierced in many places so that people will not feel rejected and unwelcome.

The Church, by its nature, is invitational, so those who have been made to feel unwelcome have been made to feel like that by people not representing the Church in its true nature. This distortion is perpetuated by Satan in order to dilute the power and impact of the Lord's redemptive act, that is, the Passion and death of Jesus. The enemy advertises the distortions aggressively, and holiness, not self-promoting by its nature, goes largely unobserved.

We must assume that many in today's society are un-churched, even if they are baptized Catholics. If we assume this, we will be less likely to be superior with others and think always of teaching the Catechism, even if it is in the smallest of doses.

Part Four

Marriage: A Unit of Mission in the World

When parents are connected securely to their matrimonial obligations, the tendency to provide formation for their children most often flows naturally. Indeed, this home, attached to the solid rock of shared vocation, becomes an oasis for spiritual formation of any children who spend time there. The matrimonial graces flow through the couple from heaven, into the family, and such is the strength of these graces that there is a surplus which flows out from each family member. As it is intended by heaven, this family becomes a unit of mission in the world. There is a well of fresh water, as it were, resting securely between the husband and wife. They protect this well through their fidelity to their marital vows.

As has been said before, when a couple is married, heaven places many hopes in that sacrament. God entrusts these hopes to the two people. His investment in the sacrament is huge and the couple has no idea of the extent to which God intends them to be a constant witness to His love through ongoing participation in the sacramental graces of their marriage.

I have seen many wells. Water flows through most of them, and yet, each well is so different. Some are sheltered and therefore have only very surface weathering wear. Others are more exposed to the elements and show more damage. Even in the case where the well itself has been very damaged by the elements, fresh clean water can come up through it as long as it remains standing and functional. There is nothing worse or more disappointing than encountering a well that looks good but draws no water, a faux well. What a sham! The only hope is that at some time in the future it will descend down into the ground and begin to produce.

My dear friends, the well is the marriage, the water is God's grace. Only if the well is secure can the water flow up through it. A marriage is sheltered by the holiness of the man and woman and God's goals are perfectly safe when there is constant striving for unity between them.

Each marriage is unrepeatable, as each person is unrepeatable. There can be a terrible temptation for couples to compare their 'well' or marriage to that of others. But no two marriages can look alike, nor does God need any two marriages to look alike. Neither should any two priests look alike nor any two religious. Single people should also contribute their individual selves to the Church, retaining their personal identity. Heaven requires diversity so that the Kingdom can come.

The graces or 'water' God sends through each matrimonial unit of mission will be unique to that marriage. God needs each couple to search for their marriage's unique heavenly identity. In a marriage, a desire for holiness in the wife plus a desire for holiness in the husband equals a very secure, very deep and very productive well for heaven. Notice I did not say holiness but a *'desire'* for holiness. This is a real desire, of course, which will include a furthering of that desire which means a commitment to a disciplined prayer life and to, at the very least, the minimum practices of the faith.

I discriminate in this way to arrest the notion that the two people must be saints. We could all be holier and if the success of the Church relied on the perfection of her children, she, the Church, would not have made it through even the First Century, never mind twenty-one centuries. God is perfect. We must simply try our best to be holy.

Now, with regard to the wells that are damaged by the elements, pockmarked, cracked in places and so forth, these wells have become exposed to injury by the lack of commitment to the sacrament by one or both people in the marriage. How vulnerable the well becomes when the parties do not focus. There must be complete abandonment to God's plan for the marriage. Each person should be a slave to the marriage, a total servant to the marriage. Each must have a spirit of submission to the well, a spirit of obedience to the structure that is the marriage.

When men are living in authentic masculinity, they will be open and welcoming to the complexity of their feminine counterparts. If what flows from a man is protection toward a woman with also a desire to provide, then his view toward her would seem well-ordered. If this includes a profound respect for the feminine strength and wisdom she possesses, another elevation in the relationship is possible. If, also, this man united in matrimony reveres the maternity and the out flowing of this maternity, this man will be the holy servant to her that heaven desires.

It must be noted that St. Joseph assumed his duties as head of household with a divinely formed and sustained methodology. Has it ever been stated that he was dominating? Controlling? Superior? No. There is no hint of this. Time has held Joseph to be a servant to Our Lady in every sense of the word. He, St. Joseph, it seems, provided Our Lady with the emotional and physical safety she required in order to be free to nurture the Savior. In a well-ordered marriage, the husband protects the space for his wife. When a woman has a child, her attention becomes directed to the infant in a powerful way. The husband, while completely involved, continues to gaze at the external world and lead accordingly to retain the safe place for his wife and children.

Some might say this is an antiquated view but I believe this is the direction of the future in that the position of the husband as head of the family will be restored to him and the position of the wife as heart of the family will be restored to her. The difference will be the equality between the genders and the acceptance of necessary exceptions of this model.

Holy Formation For All God's Children

I can see that Jesus desires holy formation for all of God's children. Parents will always be the primary formatters of their children, unless they are unavoidably separated from them. In such cases of separation, the parent must make heroic acts of trust to God, placing his or her children in the care of heaven. Ongoing petitioning of heaven should take the place of contact. How heartbreaking this experience must be but how powerfully heaven answers the pleas of a parent enduring separation.

In order to be alert to the specific needs of formation applied to the individual child, a parent must be paying attention. It is a problem in the West, for certain, and possibly in other areas of the world, that some parents continue on with their childhood even though they are adults. Some seek recreation as though they were children. In marriage, one or both parties behaving in this way will weaken the well. Water, intended for mystical hydration, is never delivered. If one person abandons the emotional, physical, or spiritual obligations to the spouse or family, the other spouse must be even holier in order to compensate. If one spouse is immature, the other must compensate by being even steadier. In most marriages, the couple will experience many different conditions. This is to be expected and unless there is danger, both should remain peacefully serving while they work toward and await an improvement in the condition of the relationship.

I believe that the focus of the marriage should be on the formation of the children if there are children. Mothers and fathers, study your children in order to adapt and adjust your formation to their constantly changing development, as well as to the external influences each child experiences. Fathers, especially, must understand this as a serious obligation for which there will be serious accountability. Men must understand that their childhood is over and the extent to which they assume their responsibilities will determine the future for their children like nothing else. Women must understand that their vocation takes priority over other elements in their life.

Expressions of Sexuality

Women, abandon vanity. Dignity is obtained through modesty and self-respect which, while including some attention to appearance, will never include an obsession with appearance. Allow God's love, compassion and kindness to flow through you to your husband and he will find you not only consoling but attractive. Examine closely the desire to be admired and examine also whether or not you are dressing to seduce. We, as females, must be certain that we are not seeking to elicit sexual desire or sexual attention from men.

As couples, we must keep our sexual energy turned toward each other. Clearly, adultery will siphon off all of the strength of the union but there is another less obvious threat than physical infidelity and that is emotional infidelity or emotional adultery.

This takes place when a married person becomes engaged in a relationship with a member of the opposite sex outside of their marriage. Perhaps this friendship begins innocently, but moves to the less innocent place of usurping one's spouse in the other's sexual and/or emotional field of vision. The third party is assigned with many of the qualities that one person feels their spouse lacks. The third party is admiring, attentive, and affectionate. This can draw the person with low self-esteem into a dangerous place because instead of advancing into wellness in the relationship at home, he or she is expending love intended for his or her spouse on the outsider. This is wasted because it cannot maintain the well or sacrament because there is no well or sacrament with the outsider. This is like painting the neighbor's house while your own becomes more and more decrepit. A flower sits dying in a pot while water is being poured onto pavement. This is very serious.

Also, a spouse senses when something he or she craves and is entitled to, that is, the attention and love of their spouse, is being denied them. This will not bring out the best in a spouse and we have a slippery patch becoming more and more treacherous. God pleads with us to be patient during times of marital difficulty.

One person cannot be two people. One person can only be one person. What I am trying to say is that if our spouse becomes distracted, we must be careful not to compound the problem by also being distracted. In the case of our spouse being distracted, we must dig in even deeper to hold the course of the family steady for heaven. There will be hurt, of course, and wounding, and there will be loneliness, but this pain should be taken to the foot of the cross each day. Jesus will whisper from the cross to the suffering spouse and instruct this spouse in the details of preserving the family, even when this is done from physical separation. In the case of abuse of a spouse or children, safety is the first consideration. And in the case of adultery, the marriage itself is at risk. Behaviors such as these do not qualify as distractions, but as aggressive and serious departures from holiness. A family struggling with these matters should seek external support to assist in making the best decisions for everyone concerned.

Dearest brothers and sisters who are hurting from the pain of family disunity, be encouraged. Trust Jesus in everything. He will protect His interests. We must trust God to what can seem like almost a ridiculous degree. If we believe God will protect us, God can work freely to the extent we trust Him to work and allow Him to work. We must let go of the project, calm ourselves, and settle into praying through what could necessarily be a long process of recovery. Has God abandoned us? Is heaven less present because our circumstances are changing or difficult? Of course not. Rather, Heaven sends ongoing strength and courage, light and consolation when the parties feel the well is crumbling.

The Desire for Holiness

I feel there is no point in talking about the ideal marriage without discussing how to maintain it, which is through, as stated, the desire for holiness in both parties. There is a supposition that a good marriage means two people totally engaged with each other with locked-in gazes, so to speak. This is wrong. This can come from an obsessive desire to use a person to fill emptiness within oneself. The person attempting this will never be satisfied. The person who is obsessive about his or her spouse will always be disappointed in the spouse because the spouse, regardless of what he or she offers, does not even possess to give what the other lacks, which is self-worth. We must try to bring a whole person into the union. Two halves do not make a whole when it comes to marriage. Two halves make a half because a marriage needs two wholes. We cannot become whole without a relationship to Jesus Christ.

Becoming the Right Person

Let us remember, single apostles, that our time is best spent becoming the right person, not trying to find the right person. Do not spend the bulk of your time looking. Spend the bulk of your time becoming. Become. If we, as single lay apostles, constantly seek to find the right person, we are not trying hard enough to become the right person. In this case, we are ignoring our need for development and the right person might not choose us because we have not cooperated with the Lord in our own formation.

Dear single apostles, work hard in the Church. Serve to the fullest extent of your capabilities. Give unselfishly to the children in your life, perhaps siblings, perhaps nieces and nephews. I feel so strongly that aunts and uncles and siblings underestimate terribly their role in the lives of the children around them.

God means business when a child is baptized and others stand with the parents. God knows the family will need to be supported during times of trial so that the children can be safe. The busier and more productive the well, the more people will come to it to drink, spiritually speaking. When people congregate at a well, they lean on it and against it, they may also kick at it or leave debris around it. Sometimes people come into the vicinity of the well who are dangerous to the structure and often a father, as head of household and protector, or a mother, as intuitive formatter, must make a decision that a person or persons are not acceptable company for their family. So be it.

Oh how heaven rejoices when men and women comply and submit to their roles in the family, supporting their spouses to the fullest extent. This beautiful exercising of the call of vocation brings so many graces to the world. St. Teresa of Avila once said, "If women were what they should be, men could be what they should be." A holy woman will draw gentle leadership from her husband. When this occurs that woman will breathe a sigh of relief and get on with her own work instead of fighting for a dominant position in the family.

Yes, when marriage is lived out with a high level of holiness, all of heaven rejoices and this unit of mission, the well, is fully utilized. Along with countless other functions, this unit of mission will provide a place of refuge for priests and religious and will become a place of lively interest in the Church and in God's work, even though the focus will be primarily on the formation and protection of the children.

This is the beautiful part of God's plan. Even with laser-like focus of this family on their children, God's grace is so plentiful and comes in such abundance through this well, that there is water for many other functions. An area of hydration will be seen around this well and those coming in steady contact with the well will also blossom.

We can sum it up by saying that each person in a marriage must be constantly reverent about God's need for his or her movement to holiness and safety. A great deal of hope is resting on the personal integrity and holiness of every single husband and every single wife. Satan can do huge damage to the Kingdom by distracting even one husband or one wife from the obligations of their vocation.

Each husband and each wife must be engaged directly with Christ and then from Christ to each other. This will ensure the correct disposition of mutual service and exquisite reverence about the protection of God's plan.

Lay people should never underestimate their importance in the Church. They direct their efforts to serving the Church at large wherever God places them. This is a distinct call and must be given the respect it deserves. But ongoing faith formation is necessary for the laity to effectively take their place. Greater reverence is needed for each vocation to be brought to its highest possible fruition.

Entering the Sacrament

With regard to marriage, formation is necessary for the couple to enter into the sacrament with full knowledge and understanding.

It is true that before marriage, many people possess romantic and idealistic visions of marriage. There is a great understanding perhaps of what one will gain from the spouse and the marriage and less understanding of what one will be asked to give to the spouse and the marriage. Marriage and getting married should be viewed as embarking on a dedicated plan of service. The two together are committing to become one unit of mission in the world, wherever that shall take them and with whatever children God sends.

How grateful God would be if engaged couples agreed in advance about the prayer life of the family. How grateful God would be if each married couple would discuss the direction of the family from a faith perspective, perhaps altering the prayer life at times as necessary when children grow older or begin to move on out of the home. One thing is certain, the formation of the children will rely upon the prayers and example of the parents.

When a parent is not setting a good example, the Lord moves to others around the child to set an example and provide critical formation. It is for this reason that extended family, friends and community must always be alert to providing good example for all children. Children will always be learning something, be it good or bad.

It is clear that addictions, particularly to alcohol, drugs or pornography, work, shopping, and gambling, grossly and seriously interfere with a parent's impact on children. If a parent is attached to a substance or sinful practice, he or she will become emotionally and spiritually unavailable. Children sense their abandonment and become agitated and afraid.

Parents, we are asking our children to make courageous and selfless choices. God needs this from them. Are we, ourselves, making courageous and selfless choices? There was a detective who worked with young people. He said, "If you want to know if the children are drinking, look at the parents. If the parents are drinking, the children are drinking." Clearly there are many exceptions attached to such a statement, however, there is also an undeniable truth attached. Children learn more from what we do then from what we say.

I want to clarify that God does not desire all marriages to look alike. On the contrary, such a thing is not even possible. I have stated this before. The Catholic Church is not an exclusive club but a universal family. A couple should feel free to achieve their unique identity within the Church. And one spouse could be powerfully attracted to a spirituality that holds no appeal for the other. This is fine.

There was once a spouse who became very excited about a certain spirituality. His wife was disinterested. This upset the man but he obtained wise counsel which steered him toward living the spirituality as opposed to talking the spirituality. Several months elapsed. Finally, the wife asked for the spiritual readings her husband loved so much, stating, "I could ignore the spirituality, but I could not ignore the changes it brought about in my husband." God used this particular spirituality to refresh and renew the unit of mission that was this family. He did not do this through an imposition of a spirituality from one spouse to another, but through a softening of one spouse, a greater humility of one spouse. People, particularly spouses, are more likely to be influenced by humanity and tenderness than talk, talk, and more talk. Only by living the spirituality, will we become qualified to preach it.

Protecting the Family

Thursday July 22, 2010

It can occur that a family veers off the track of holiness. Dear apostles, this is very serious. Perhaps there is an addiction or many addictions or perhaps there is abuse. Perhaps there is disconnection between the spouses. Perhaps the family has become lukewarm or perhaps the family possesses a worldly view that encourages material success without holy purpose. There can be many crosses in a family, to be sure, but crosses do not detract from holiness and most families will carry some cross or crosses over time. But a general goal of aiming toward heaven will insulate the family from moral danger. If the aim is off, the family as a unit of mission becomes unsustainable. Heaven has difficulty protecting that which refuses her protection.

Think of a lifeguard. A lifeguard watches closely. He knows where he can protect people. He also knows that if people go outside of the safe barrier, he may not be able to prevent them from getting into trouble. They, through their own decision to behave foolishly, place themselves at risk of being unreachable in distress. They are not heeding the lifeguard's safety parameters. The lifeguard knows what he is doing and he has watched the waters, day after day. He has watched people perish because they ignore the safety guidelines.

My friends, God is the lifeguard. The beach is life and the water is behavior.

People complain that the Catholic Church has too many 'rules.' If one studies the teachings of our faith, one will find the teachings to be protective in nature. To swim outside of the safety barriers is to knowingly abandon the teachings. The danger may not be apparent at once but if a storm comes or a swimmer simply becomes tired, as one does in life, he will not be able to put his feet down to rest because he has abandoned the area of foundation. He is, you see, in over his head. In those cases, many call out to God and He pulls them back to safety but damage is done in many ways, to both themselves and others because a bad example has a similar ripple effect to a good example.

In terms of families, we can see a sad pattern in some units of mission. Marriage, as a sacramental union, should possess a heavenly bearing. Without this bearing, two people can be drifting at sea. This can happen when parents are reluctant to behave like adults. Some say, 'work hard, play hard,' but playing is for children. Working is for adults. Adults should not think in terms of excessive recreation with or without their family. This cannot be a good thing. Once childhood is over, play time is over. There should always be light playful hearts, of course. God wants this and God Himself gives this to His followers, but there must be a serious spirit of service to the spouse and the children.

Many people come to a place in their time on earth where they know they have to alter course, their own perhaps, but also that of their family. This is excellent. Changes must be made everywhere and at the very least, if there is not family prayer, then family prayer must begin and that all alone is a change. Often, it is pain which prompts the decision to change the course and a good idea would be to alter the course of the family if the course is off. That stated, a parent who has been morally absent but who converts and then decides to change everybody else is working on the wrong person. The person who recognizes that the family is off course must change him or herself first. Then, after the example is consistent for a time, this person can begin loving outreach to the others. I cannot stress this enough.

There is nothing worse than witnessing someone who has behaved badly and ignored responsibilities, converting and focusing entirely on the flaws of his or her family members. Nobody likes this person. Truly, this person has no credibility and that is why there must be a consistent example of conversion before the family will recognize a genuine shift in the wind.

Also, in these situations, one spouse may be ready for change long before the other, or one spouse has grown so weary of seeking change that he or she has given up. Dear apostles, God understands the dreadful fatigue that comes from past disappointment. God understands the exhaustion that comes with an unhealthy marital relationship. But if we could see the hope God has in our marriages, for the world, we would only separate for the most serious matters. And even in these matters, there is sometimes hope of reconciliation. It can be very difficult to sort things out without an outsider who is objective, so some form of Christian-based marriage counseling would be appropriate far before anyone leaves. Our marriages are important and good decisions in the beginning will provide ongoing insulation for the sacrament.

Love Your Spouse Through Christ

July 23, 2010

In marriage we remember that we are always moving, as individuals first, then as couples and families. This is why the direction in which we are moving is so vital. If we are moving away from heaven, we will see sadness and suffering throughout the family. If we are moving toward heaven, we will see growth in virtue and character. There are many romantic ideas about marriage and love. In a Catholic marriage or indeed any Christian marriage, it is true that each person must have a personal relationship with Christ and then love their spouse through Christ. How is this different?

First and foremost, a relationship with Christ helps us to take things less personally. When we are hurt, we take the hurt to Christ, who softens the pain and then directs us back to the relationship with a disposition that seeks to first self-examine and next to resolve the conflict. When we have a personal relationship with Christ, the bulk of our pain is dealt with there.

Every married person will be able to give a full account of

how it feels to be the victim of injustice. There can be squabbles over who is working harder, who is sacrificing more and which person is assuming more of the family workload than the other. This is necessary if the couple is to work as a team. Every few months or so, the picture of the family must be studied, if only briefly. Usually it is conflict which prompts this scrutiny so we should never be alarmed that there is conflict. Any time people are working together as a team, there will be a need for conflict resolution. If there are children in the home, the parents are teaching lessons to the children about resolving conflict that these children will take into their own families. We are teaching our children how to be husbands and wives. We, parents, must be keenly aware that we are always modeling marriage for our children.

Because this is true, we want our children to learn how to be kind to their spouse, even when there is hurt. We want our children to learn to honor prayer commitments, even when family life is tumultuous. We want our children to know that the home should be a safe place, both physically and emotionally and also spiritually. Children should hear the name of God referenced regularly as a reason why certain decisions are being made as opposed to other decisions. Children should come to know how Jesus speaks to others through the conversation of his parents, that is, gentle and loving.

These are high standards, one might observe. People, especially people challenged with financial, emotional or mental issues, or even just 'stress of life' issues, are not likely to be able to meet this standard each day. This is true and realistic. And that is why children must hear the words, "I'm sorry" in their home. They must understand the need for humble reconciliation in times of distress and the words "I love you" over and over, like so many benedictions on the relationships of the home.

So, contrary to many romantic notions, marriage is not a locked-in relationship which pushes out individuality but a blessed friendship where each person, united with Christ, comes to the other as a fellow traveler on the road of service and holiness.

Dealing with Difficulties in Your Marriage

Yes, romantic idealizations depict marriage as two people totally absorbed in each other. While there is some of this in the beginning, what emerges should be two people totally and separately absorbed in Christ through their service to each other and their other family members. Self-identity with Christ is necessary and wholesome. A personal relationship with Christ is not a threat to the intimacy in the relationship of husband and wife. It is a reality, a perfect truth. We will not account for our sins as a team, dear friends, even though we sometimes commit sin with another person or persons. Our part of the sin will travel with us to the next world if we do not repent.

Many times a husband or wife behaves badly. I suppose really, in life, this will be unavoidable. Lay apostles, be alert here. Do not use the bad behavior of your spouse or anyone else to justify your own bad behavior. Let us say our spouse behaves badly and speaks in an unkind way. What is the temptation? To respond in kind and also speak in an unkind way. Will God then say when you arrive in the next life, "Please give me a full account of everything your spouse did wrong during your marriage." Clearly not. God knows what your spouse has done wrong. God is with you in your suffering. It is more likely that God will say, "Let us together face your successes and failures."

Often there is more serious trouble in marriages when one or the other more or less abandons his or her obligations to the spouse or children. They will use many things to justify their neglect including inflating charges against the spouse. In these cases, the other spouse will face serious temptation. There will be a temptation to join the party and also abandon holiness and obligation. There will be a temptation to become bitter and seek 'I deserve it' consolation elsewhere, in material things, questionable friendships with members of the opposite sex or even addictions. This is very important, dear apostles. Regardless of the behavior of our spouse, we are called to be holy. We are never more called to return love for hostility than when our spouse misbehaves. We must concentrate acutely on our personal holiness, on the most saintly response in each moment to each situation. I have seen many husbands and wives 'join the party' so to speak as a way to eliminate their own loneliness at being emotionally abandoned, but this only results in the whole thing shifting. If one person of the two can remain fixed in a holy relationship with Christ, the children will be as protected as possible and will come out right in the end. Holy companionship is absolutely necessary for a spouse whose partner has lost focus or whose spouse never had focus.

Giving Children a Catholic Identity

Identity is important. Both adults and children must know who they are and where they come from. Parents, it is true that we want our children taking their identity as

Catholics out into the world and influencing others. The opposite of this would be our children lacking Catholic identity and going out into the world only to be influenced by others who lack a Catholic identity. We, parents in the home, are primary formatters of our children. We must, particularly as mothers, consider that we are providing spiritual formation just as a Mother Superior is providing spiritual formation in a religious order.

Mothers, be on guard to anything that tempts you from this most holy obligation. Be with your children as much as possible while they are young because that is when we have the opportunity to provide them with this identity, with this formation, helping them to identify and acquire the virtues. Each night, when the children are going to bed, it is good to admire some little thing they did in the day, some little service, some act of kindness, some triumph over temptation. There is always something that can be given to them as a gift and let the children, as they fall asleep, contemplate their huge capacity for good. This will console them and they will rest in the dignity they deserve as children of Goodness.

Fathers, moral leadership of the family is your special call. Making moral decisions in the little things teaches integrity and keeps the family secure. The children will then know that they are departing from something if they make decisions against integrity. If integrity is lacking, the children are simply following the path that has been marked out for them by deciding against truth and honesty in their own lives. Dear parents, do not be surprised when your children make mistakes similar to your own. We have all seen this. Fathers, above all, remain sober in your practices. Hold yourself to a high but not impossible standard and be compassionate as Christ is compassionate. If your wife is loved and knows she is your priority, the chance of her wandering into bad behavior will be lessened. Children feel so safe when a father loves their mother.

Because we are called to be a light to all nations, we must live our Catholic faith with constancy and seriousness. If formation is lacking in our homes, our children will be formed by other adults, television and modern culture. This cannot be a good thing, either for our children or for the world. God hopes that our children will be formed in the teachings of our Church to influence the world, not the other way around. Consider it this way.

Someone is always forming your children. Is it you?

Choose Wisely

Young men and women of God, choose wisely. Ask yourself if the person you are dating is willing to view marriage through the eyes of Christ, never mind living it out that way. If the person you are dating does not share this sacramental view of marriage, how can we expect him or her to exercise it later? If the person you are dating does not view the formation of children with the most reverent sense of responsibility, how can we expect them to exercise it fully as a parent? Such cruel disappointment God's children experience in unwise marriages, and yet, such humility from suffering and such miraculous healing of many marital unions.

Single people, perhaps you feel you are called to the married state and you are with a person and you are not sure if this person is suitable for marriage. Perhaps you are asking yourself if you are with the right person. This will always be a deeply personal decision, of course, but light can be shed with the following considerations.

First of all, there should be attraction, what is commonly known as chemistry. We can say that if there is no chemistry, this is probably not the right person, but we can also say that the fact that there is chemistry does not guarantee this is the right person. Chemistry is the very beginning of a relationship, not the sum total. We will be attracted to many people in the course of our lifetime. Being attracted does not mean we share ourselves sexually. Also, lust must be separated from chemistry. Hmm. How can we distinguish the two?

Lust will always be directed toward self, not other. Lust will prompt using, not reverencing. Lust will draw one away from one's life path, not further into it. Lust will prompt disrespect, not respect. Lust will eventually make us feel unsafe emotionally, instead of emotionally safe. Lust will make us view our duties as tedious. Lust will be settling for anything, as opposed to striving for everything.

Still, chemistry and attraction should be in the relationship, for certain. This is the beginning.

Next, we look at ourselves to determine if we are with the right person. Are we what we should be spiritually? Are we practicing our faith and proceeding as a Catholic single person? If we are not, we have to question whether or not we are in the right spirit to make a decision about who we are going to serve alongside for the rest of our lives. It would be good to get ourselves in the right place, that is, return to our faith practice and ask Jesus to help us to be what we should be and then ask Jesus to be with us in our process of discernment about our future spouse.

Another consideration is how we feel in the relationship. Are we free to be our very best selves? Are we comfortable expressing our faith and spirituality? Is there any feeling that if we expressed our real selves, that is, our best selves, spiritually or any other way, this person would reject us? There is nothing lonelier than being with a person and not being free to be our true self. This leads to terrible isolation and emotional aching.

Yet another consideration is very basic. Is this person practicing his or her faith? Does this person show signs that he or she has participated in his or her own faith journey? If the faith journey of your potential spouse is beginning, we thank God and have the highest of hopes but we must also be certain that this potential spouse shows a capacity for ongoing spirituality and growth. Is this person willing to respect your ongoing conversion and participate in his own? Will this person help you to teach respect for God and our Church to your children? Could you see this person working against you in this regard? Be alert if you detect sarcasm about faith or a sarcastic view of the Church. This will be a bad sign. Cynicism is another symptom that humility is lacking. Dear single Catholics, so precious to God, please be alert about this and ask God to help you to be honest with yourself. We do not expect our future spouses to be saints, of course, but they should be open to the faith and they should possess humility.

In the case of marriage to someone from a different faith, there must be a great deal of conversation about how you as a couple will proceed spiritually and this must be done before the marriage takes place.

Also, it would be good to examine your potential spouse's expectations with regard to gender roles. Are these expectations similar to yours? Is there flexibility? Is there a general match-up in the way you both wish to proceed in this regard? If the potential spouse has a view that is very different from your own, there will be trouble if the issues are not ironed out in advance.

Now we deal with another very important issue. Has any member of your family or close friend expressed concerns to you about your relationship with this person? Clearly, when we say family and close friends we are speaking of people close to you who love you and are credible and reasonably clear-sighted. If people who fit this description are concerned about this relationship, you should be, too. Family can get it wrong, of course, but it is very important to consider their observations and warnings. How many family members have watched a loved one enter into a marriage that they knew was doomed to cause pain and hardship? This is a great cross indeed for family members.

Dear single apostles, if your family has objections or concerns about this relationship, you should not only be open to hearing them, but to acting upon them. At the very least, listen carefully and embark upon a closer scrutiny, with Christ.

It would hardly seem to be necessary to make the next statement but sometimes we must re-master the obvious. Do not marry someone who has an addiction to alcohol, drugs, gambling or pornography. Let the addiction be addressed first, at the barest minimum, acknowledged. Let there be some agreement about the addiction in advance so a spouse has leverage if, in the marriage, the addiction rears its head.

Men, use of pornography is not acceptable. Women, use of pornography is not acceptable. Catholics, Jesus wants you to remove all pornography from your life, at once. Ask God for a great grace of recovery if you have used pornography. Pornography has nothing to do with a healthy sexual relationship. It is a sin that compounds itself, again and again, according to how many people view it or participate in it later. Do not cooperate with pornography in any way.

Being filmed or photographed in an unhealthy manner, meaning, without clothes on or while acting sexually, even for strictly personal use, will never be a good thing. Please do not be talked into such a thing. Sexual expression is meant to be in the now, not physically memorialized. It is a deeply personal expression and should be treated as such, with reverence and privacy.

This is a whole writing in itself but perhaps we can leave it at this: Pornography and the use of pornography will always be a threat to a healthy sexual relationship between two people, as well as a threat to an individual's relationship with God.

An apostle should remember that the Confessional graces cleanse and purify. The past is the past. Accept with joy the hand of the Savior as He continually directs you to face forward, away from past mistakes. Reject the sexual shaming offered by God's enemy.

To summarize, are you making a decision to marry that is consistent with and welcoming of your Catholic faith? Are you both practicing your faith? Are you generally in agreement about how you will proceed as a couple with regard to the big issues, that is, children, careers and use of substances? Are there any large concerns about the relationship by your loved ones? Are you free to be yourself or do you find yourself constantly trying to gain the approval of your potential spouse in ways that are not consistent with who you are when you are with your family and loved ones? Are you confident about saying no to any sexual expression that makes you uncomfortable? Are you in love in a way that makes you want to serve in the marriage, building a holy place where God is welcome and where He can use you together as a couple to love each other and be a part of a greater Christian community in the world? This is what we embark upon when we decide for marriage. Our Church helps us with teachings such as Natural Family Planning and Theology of the Body.

I sense that there are married people reading this and saying, "I had no idea I was getting into something that serious." And yet, God draws us along in our marriages. If we are faithful at all, God forms and creates, and God has His way in our homes. Many say that married people begin to look alike after a time. This is so beautiful because it means there is harmony. How beautiful is the beauty of a mature marriage. This communication of love and unity between the two reflects heaven, just as it should.

Dear young apostles who desire marriage, look for examples of successful marriage and study them. What is it you admire? Strive for these characteristics in your dating relationships and you will know when holy interactions are possible and when holy interactions are not possible. You will then have your answer on whether or not you are with the right person.

Parenting in Unexpected Circumstances

Lay apostles, we have all seen or experienced situations where a marriage breaks down, sometimes temporarily but sometimes permanently. Our Church provides pastoral support in many different ways. In terms of the family, we often then see two parents providing formation from separate locations. In the best of circumstances, the parents are able to separate their differences from their formation of the children and we have unity about parenting. This is very important to the children so any effort that goes into creating a peaceful situation for children of separated or divorced parents is effort well spent. Divorce being what it is, this may not always be possible but God will be omnipresent, have no fear. Again I say to trust God in the face of every circumstance and He will bring the children right as soon as possible.

When a person is parenting alone, regardless of the circumstances, Jesus Himself stands behind the single parent to provide a solid place for support and encouragement. It is lonely, parenting alone, but I would ask the single parent to remember that it is far lonelier to be parenting with a violent or disruptive partner than it is to be parenting alone.

Dear parent, I know you are lonely but Jesus loves our children far more than we do and if He has entrusted them to us, He will help us to both provide for them and fashion them according to His plan.

In the case of single parenting, Catholic identity is even more crucial. Our children will retain perfect dignity if we connect them to the Church as we are bringing them up through their childhood. Jesus Christ and our Blessed Mother view all children as treasures, irreplaceable to the Kingdom of God. Therefore, if these children are secure in their place in the Church, they will be secure in their place in the world. I have seen many children from single-parent families flourishing. They generally, like all children, adapt to the viewpoint of the parent so the parent must be vigilant about his or her own dignity. This means, dear parents, conducting ourselves rightly and not exposing the children to any influences that are in conflict with holy formation. Children will not do what we say. Children will do what we do.

The call to holy formation extends to all parents, regardless of their condition or circumstances. Dear parents, we are all on our own faith journey. None of us has reached perfect holiness. This is no excuse to delay formation of our children. I speak with great sincerity and compassion. I speak from the Lord's heart. If you are addicted to drugs and alcohol, you should still be attempting to provide holy formation for your children. If you are living with a person without benefit of the sacrament of marriage, you should still be attempting to provide holy formation for your children. If you experience same-sex attraction and you are in a relationship, perhaps living with a partner of the same gender, you should still be attempting to provide holy formation for your children. If you are married, and your marriage is not happy, you should still be attempting to provide holy formation for your children.

Addictions tear at everyone in the family and we must all pray for healing for those addicted to the many substances and habits that distract us from our duties. We, parents, should all be terrified of the impact of addictions on our children.

With regard to the other circumstances of families who are living in irregular unions, do not wait until your life is perfect to catechize your children. The Catechism calls for an 'apprenticeship of self mastery' regarding chastity. God is with you and loves you. God understands your circumstances. He expects the need for process and movement to holiness. In this situation, the aim would be to live as brother and sister until former marriages are annulled and a new union blessed. It is often the case that one of the two is willing to do this and the other is not. This can cause discord and be discouraging. Don't be discouraged! Recognize the call and ask God to help and then use the confessional as a refuge of forgiveness and strength.

With regard to those in relationships with someone of the same gender, understand that God is heavily invested in your holiness. The Kingdom of God craves your presence for its coming. God rejoices in all of your goodness and recognizes your desire to help Him through your good works and your love for each other and those around you. God understands you perfectly. We Christians share a universal call to chastity. We are all together in this. You are not called to reject love or to live without love or without those you love. Perhaps, like the rest of us, it will be a process for you. If God allows for heterosexuals to make mistakes and experience His forgiveness in the sacramental graces of the Confessional, it is certain he allows the same for those who experience same-sex attraction. Do not delay your movement toward joyful holiness for any reason. Fr. John Harvey's book *Homosexuality and the Catholic Church* examines the truth of these matters and the Courage apostolate is a life-giving source of comfort and encouragement for those seeking the Church's teachings.

Regardless of your circumstances, go to Mass. Do your best to love each other and your children. Submit your family to God and ask for His help. God welcomes you and your children into the Church. You may say, "Yes, but others do not welcome us." Well, the important thing is that God welcomes you and He is working as quickly as He can with others. Come back to your faith in humility and teach your children about Jesus. Many people go to Mass for years and do not receive the Eucharist because they are not conforming to the Church teaching in some area. These people must be commended for their respect and love for God's presence in the Magisterium. Imagine how grateful God is that they do not give up on Him. Imagine how moved God is that they respect the teachings enough to make spiritual communions instead of sacramental communions. This means, to be specific, you would not receive Holy

Communion. Instead you ask Jesus to spiritually enter your heart. Many people do this for years.

We, as lay apostles, always defer to the teaching of the Catechism with regard to the Eucharist which states that we do not receive Holy Communion unless we are in a state of grace but never avoid Mass because you are not going to receive Communion.

Dear friends, resist any temptations to bitterness. The reality is that each one of us has our own difficulties in trying to live up to the fullness of our Church's beautiful teachings. Jesus wants us in the Church family as we struggle toward perfection. I know many who are in situations through very little fault of their own. It is not God who closes doors against them but God's enemy and in the case of your children, get them to Jesus!!! They need Him and He wants them in His care.

Also, you are needed in the Church. Others will look at your example and come back, too, because of your courage. Others will see that you are forming your children according to Catholic teaching and they will have the example to follow. You are so important! The decisions you make with regard to your children's formation are not only crucial to your children but to the children of many others. Come back now, dear friends. Your Church needs your help. Your family is called to be a unique unit of mission in the world.

Perhaps you do not want to attend a Catholic Church because you believe someone in the Catholic Church does not accept you but be assured, Jesus wants you there.

Lay apostles, if you know people living in these circumstances, please be certain to invite them back into our faith if they have gone away from it. Do not feel you have to make explanations you are not sure about. Say simply, "God loves you and He wants you in His Church." Then, leave the explanations to a priest or lay person who is qualified to lovingly support the person with more detailed information and direction. We do not have to be experts in the Catechism to love. We have to be experts in love to love. God is an expert in love. The Holy Spirit is an expert in love. Jesus Christ, on whom we model ourselves, is an expert in love. So if we are experts in love we will represent Christ accurately. And when you fear that you are directing people into a Church that does not welcome them, you must say to yourself, "I am directing people to Jesus Christ, truly present in the Eucharist and I am directing people into the stream of living grace that comes from the sacraments." People will always be changeable but Jesus Christ never changes.

Families with Members Who Have Disabilities

Just as no two families are alike, so no two family members are alike. Each family must have reverence for each family member and the unrepeatable role of each family member. Sometimes it occurs that a member of the family experiences a disability. At first glance, parents told that their child is disabled can experience many emotions. This can be terrifying for parents because of the fear they experience about protecting their children! A parent generally assumes that his or her children will be young for a time, during which the parents will provide protection and formation and then the parent expects the child to become independent. In the case of some disabilities the expectation is removed because the family member will be unable to become independent.

Most parents feel, upon gazing at their newly born

children, that they would be willing to die for them if some malevolent force threatened. This instinct to protect must be translated from a willingness to die for the person to a readiness to live for the person. Most of us will not be called upon to die to for our children, but all of us are called to die to self, so that our children can have what they need. Never more is this true than when we are first told that our child has a disability. Many things happen in that moment and each of us as parents of a special needs child experiences this differently. However, one thing is for sure. We die to the world to some degree in this circumstance and everything in our life begins to reconfigure. The horizon shifts, then rights, then shifts again. Acceptance comes in waves as Plan A, the plan we had for a healthy child, moves to Plan B, or C, or D or E or F. Family beliefs, goals and priorities must also be reconfigured. Protecting one's child takes on a whole new meaning and includes different threats entirely.

At the same time, depending on the disability, some threats become neutralized. Often, there is no moral threat because many disabled people are protected from moral danger, meaning they lack the intellectual or spiritual capacity for sin. They are not accountable. Families with disabled children are blessed in so many ways. Because of this disability, they are compelled to think differently. God grants opportunity for profound graces, profound holiness, and profound vision for families who are home to one of God's children with a disability.

Remember, dear parents, "normal" does not guarantee "ok" or "safe," and "normal" absolutely does not guarantee holy.

We must parent the treasures God sends and rely on Him to send a package of grace, tailored for parenting each child, that we must open in the morning when we say our

Allegiance Prayer. The grace is in the day. The very great problem with parenting the disabled is that fear of the future can suck up all of the joy of today. Never is it more necessary to, while preparing prudently for a child's future, rejoice in the person in the present moment. Some moments are easier and more conducive to rejoicing, of course, but the difficult and scary moments will always pass into more manageable moments.

How many people suffering have learned that sometimes all that is possible is an act of endurance, waiting in the certainty that because all life is fluid, is constant motion, each particular moment of suffering will end.

The Kingdom of God within each person, draws graces for the Kingdom of God in other persons. When grace is being drawn from us, we can experience suffering from it. This suffering takes many forms and often this is experienced as a disability.

Parents, siblings, aunts and uncles, and those who care for the disabled, be alert to all that you can learn, all of the grace possible which emerges from God's children suffering a disability. Drink greedily from the possibilities that come with service to our disabled brothers and sisters. We allow God through our contact with the disabled to move us to greater heavenly vision and out of the limitations of worldly vision.

Lay apostles, look carefully around the families in your life. Are there one or two or three families who are providing a home for one of heaven's treasures? Can you provide loving support to this family? Perhaps through prayer, perhaps through encouragement, or perhaps through friendship and listening. Consider what is normal to this family and be willing to share in that normality, whatever that is. I know so many priests who do this beautifully that I must single them out as Christ-bearers to the disabled. How grateful are the families of disabled persons to have the occasional presence of priests and any others who will be part of their experience, both the joy and suffering.

It is always so educational to watch the way children deal with the disabilities of other children. They are curious, sympathetic and interested in the ramifications of the disability. And then they get on with the relationships as best they can, if they can. Also, there is no more sympathetic audience for suffering than there is from another sufferer. Fellowship is important, whatever form that takes depending on the particular disability.

Family Wealth

Families proceeding from a solid Christian identity will be careful about their views of material possessions. If a family has been given or allowed great wealth, that family will be alert to keep possessions in their proper perspective, meaning emphasize people, not things, and teach their children good stewardship. The word "wealth" is highly subjective of course. The poorest family can perceive themselves as wealthy if they compare "down" to those who have less. The wealthiest family can feel bitter if they compare "up" to those who have more. A healthy attitude for any family will be to promote an outpouring of gratitude to God for whatever blessings they have been given—material, spiritual or relational. A positive approach to our faith will teach our children to flow out from Christ generously. As an example, because we believe that God is the author of life and that each life is precious and willed by God, we will teach our children to value life, by understanding that abortion is wrong, of course, and contributing to the support of mothers who face challenging circumstances.

Parents, we teach our children to be always for something, rather than always against something. We must be a positive force in the world, drawing others into the stream of goodness and the stream of the emerging Church rather than a negative force which will mark our children as superior and contemptuous. Always compassion, always mercy, always gratitude. Do we want our children to live in the truth, which is that they have experienced some suffering but also many blessings and gifts? Let us not transmit to our children that they are entitled to greater wealth or privilege than others. This would be untrue. If our children have been blessed with steady shelter, sustenance and safety, then we expect them to flourish, assuming we parents are pouring love and formation into them which promotes Christian growth, and we expect them to then go out into the world and help others.

We aim our children toward service, not acquisition of ever greater wealth! Dear parents, we do not under-respect the need for our children to be prepared to support their families, but we do impose upon them a civic, humanitarian and spiritual obligation. The questions that should be asked are, "How is your prayer life?" and, "How are you contributing to the coming of God's Kingdom?"

For many of us, serving simply in our families and jobs, practicing our faith and loving those around us while we strive to grow in holiness will be as much as God is asking. But our children must also be open to additional calls in their vocations, to heroic commitment to our Church or to God's merciful service to humanity, perhaps far from home. Parents let us insure through proper formation of our children, that they are open to God's plan with their hearts inclined to His voice within their souls. How many parents have struggled to accept God's plan for their children when the child himself or herself has accepted it fully. Yes, I can see that we parents must respect God's Spirit in the hearts of our children and support whatever plan the Spirit dictates for them. If the child has been willing to discern a given plan, then we must be open to accepting that discernment, which will bring the child to perhaps determination as opposed to defiance.

Respecting our child's independence is not the same as abandoning our children, regardless of their age. We should accept that when our child comes to us, even as an adult, they will need us to parent, regardless of their age. We remain alert to offer guidance, albeit very gently, but nevertheless fully present to them in the ongoing responsibility of our role of mother or father.

Part Five

The Feminine Influence in the Church

In the past, inequality between the genders created a need for movement to greater equality. This elevation in the dignity of women and their contribution to political systems, government and indeed the world was a necessary step to correct lopsided advances.

If men are brave trailblazers then women make the trail a safe and comfortable place on which to journey. In heaven, there is no conflict or imbalance between the genders. None whatsoever. It must be said that gender, while retained in heaven in terms of unique identity, is no barrier to perfect equality between all people. To relieve any rigid notions, let me say that some women will be more suited to trail blazing. They will blaze trails with their femininity intact, however it evolves. Perhaps we can consider our gender, masculine or feminine, like the way we drive.

It is possible that the Church is porous right now because of her suffering. Porous might look vulnerable to some people but I do not think the Church is remotely vulnerable. I think that porous means, at this time, prepared for infusion. The infusion necessary is the feminine influence. It bears repeating that there is no heavenly conflict between men and women. Any conflict will come from the humanity of the people involved, and, as in any endeavor that includes humanity, there will be conflict. If we can all admit to our humanity, and therefore our likeliness to be wrong at times, we will move more smoothly into the stream of the Church that emerges in its ongoing call to conversion and holiness.

When we think infusion, let us think in terms of complete and utter infusion. Saturation, in fact. The feminine influence, soothing and gentle, spreads through the Church and makes her a more comfortable place to journey for all pilgrims. She will be warmer, more accessible, with a wide and welcoming front porch.

Does this mean that women should launch themselves at existing authority and embark on a wrestling match for power? Of course not. If there is no conflict, then there is no need for engaging in a fight. Obviously some struggle will occur but as in every change and every advance, struggle, with love, fuels the forward movement. Nobody should panic when they view aberrations of the infusion. Aberrations tend to set up camp alongside the stream and build their own encampment. Look for obedience to the Magisterium in order to discriminate between what is dangerous and what is benign. What is good and destined by God moves steadily along in the divine will and the Church emerging absorbs God's plan.

While we are infusing the Church with the feminine influence, we are also claiming for both men and women the full power and challenge of their gender. The feminine will not allow her maternal identity to be stripped from her. Rather, she will insist on her divine right and obligation to nurture her children, biological, adopted, or assigned. She must not be cruelly separated from her maternity. She will use the maternity to also soothe, love, and influence the men whom God wills walk alongside her. This includes men from every vocation.

The priesthood must also inhale deeply from its sisters so that it can become more complete. Ongoing relationships for priests with holy women will protect vocations, as opposed to endangering them. Authentic holiness will differ from false piety in that there will be no actions evident by the woman that threaten either the priest's purity or his commitment to duty. The monastic call is obviously distinct.

September 9, 2010

It is true that women must take their place alongside their brothers in the Church. Women have always done this, of course, but the bride of Christ continues with her nuptial preparation, therefore, ongoing adornment is appropriate, a bow here, a flower there, all beautifying the Church and moving her forward in time and in completeness.

Complimentarity between the genders is a reality. We search for this in truth and righteousness. The call to feminine leadership is one that is as compelling as the call to masculine leadership. If we could erase emotion from this and advance with only a sincere desire to do God's will, we would advance more quickly. Women who sincerely desire to do God's will have been in no way hampered by being a woman in the Church. On the contrary, many have worked to the utmost and many continue to do so. Some call women slaves in the Church but a mother will always be a slave to her family. The term slave is meant to connote mistreatment of course, and communicates a certain bitterness and aggressiveness. This is most assuredly not the way forward. Our brothers do not deserve such treatment and will not recognize the legitimate call of heaven to concede active participation to their feminine counterparts if they hear a caustic demand accompanied by aberrant spirituality, as opposed to an illumination gently shared, accompanied by authentic holiness. Yes, a gentle urging is always more successful than an aggressive and self-righteous insistence. Who is fully righteous, after all, but God Himself?

Clearly, those who hear the call to advance the authority of women in the Church must be identifying God's desires. We rejoice in the shared call and respect the commitment that is found in those who herald the future. And of course, as we know that humanity is flawed, we understand that this call will not always be accompanied by perfect representation of the call. Perhaps the direction is being heralded correctly, but often without the correct disposition and road map. We may know that Dublin is the destination and that it is to the North of us but have absolutely no idea how to get there.

I believe this is the way with those who make demands upon Church leadership to ordain women to the priesthood. This is not the way to arrive at the destination. This is what you could call taking a wrong turn. And our greatest concern, as a faith family, should be to first and foremost protect the God-given obligations of the feminine created beings and defend her role. Acknowledging, reclaiming, shaping, perfecting and all the while advancing.

It is disturbing to see women who have abandoned their feminine obligations, whatever that looks like for the individual, and grappling for power when they are unwilling to do the work the Lord has arranged for them, given their personal gifts. Nobody likes the one who goes around the house complaining about washing the floor when washing the floor is their job. Better to wash the floor joyfully while singing praises to the Lord for the privilege of being asked to work in the house. I deliberately use the image of washing the floor because if it is repugnant to the reader, the reader does not understand the concept of service. A servant will do what is being asked, even as a slave will abandon all self-will to the Master. Also, if a woman is not willing to take direction from a man in leadership, she will also rebel at taking direction from a woman in leadership, and she is certainly not fit for leadership herself because a leader, if leading for God, is a servant. Yes, a true Christian leader becomes smaller and smaller even though the job can sometimes become bigger and bigger. God will be merciful and obscure the bigness of

His plan for His chosen leaders if they are at risk of pride. That would include all of us, of course.

For the sake of truth, we distinguish power from authority. Authority equals obligation to lead. If the authority is righteous, it understands that it has no power. Those invested with authority should be acutely aware of the possibility of pride and arrogance and what comes from these things, that is, abuse of power as well as ridiculousness.

Women in the Church, be little. If we as women believe this is bad advice, then we must go more deeply into prayer. Men should feel our love and support, our encouragement and admiration. Men should not feel threatened but protected in our presence. They should feel, 'Truly, my sister will stand by me when I need her. I can rely on her fidelity to me'.

Men, make way and facilitate, always in union with the rightful authority of the Pope, the forward momentum of the feminine leadership in the Church. Love your sisters. Admire their contribution with the understanding that you are only one half of the Body of Christ and understand that for completeness we absolutely require feminine direction and support.

This is all happening and this is good.

Part Six

Welcoming Young People
in the Church

Often it is said that there are not enough young people in our Church. Many bemoan the fact that a large number of young Catholics have fallen away. There are many reasons for this, of course, some obvious and some not so obvious. To call attention to the not so obvious will be most helpful. Is it possible that the youth, with their distinct calls and distinct struggles for holiness, are not welcomed? Is it possible that those of us who are older feel superior to them in the mistaken notion that we ourselves never had to advance from childhood? Were we born mature or did we make our way into maturity with God's merciful help?

Oh dear. I am afraid we have a problem here and that is that we talk about welcoming young Catholics but, as in the case of divorced people, people who experience same-sex attraction and others, we are less good at actually doing it. It can happen that when a young person is adapting a singularly superficial piety, that person is deemed pleasing. When a young person is authentic in his or her search, that person is stamped as troublesome. Working with youth requires a charism, it is true, but loving them and encouraging them should be a reflex, like breathing. Perhaps while we allow for the struggles of young people we could also pray that they will forgive our intolerance and superiority. Who has not seen young people criticized mercilessly by people who were not remotely as holy when they were at the same age? Our youth are often so disrespected that it is, at times, astonishing.

If we are to have renewal, then we must welcome young people and allow for their struggles. Misrepresentations of the faith drive young people away, again and again, and the young detect hypocrisy from one thousand miles and flee. Who can blame them? Jesus would not do this. Jesus would draw them in and form them lovingly, as opposed to studying them for flaws as if they were rare birds. Many vocations die on the vine for want of watering. Are we watering the young people around us? Or shining a harsh light upon them that makes them shrivel? One thing is certain. We will not achieve any advance into renewal without the spirit and strength of God's young people. If we continue to get that wrong, nothing else will count for much very soon.

Just as we do not have to abandon the Catechism in order to love others, so we do not have to abandon truth to form our youth. We should not tiptoe around areas where they are mistaken, but we should respectfully and humbly praise them in the areas where they are advancing. Correction should be given briefly and honestly. One sentence. Two sentences. Clarification, if necessary. Patience in the face of backlash. And then a swift movement forward in service.

Once a mistake is identified and acknowledged, the person can be comforted and distracted by his success and potential. A formula might look like this: Less of that and more of this, please, and then on to the next thing. And then check back and see if the lesson was taken correctly and if the spirit has been willing to accept the teaching. All of this is assuming you are being asked to provide formation, in the sense of a parent or superior.

In most cases when working with young people in the Church, we will simply be called to love them and rejoice in their great gifts. Only in the absence of proper leadership should one offer correction. In the cases where there is evidence of spiritual risk and even danger, an apostle should first communicate to the person who has charge over the young person. That sentence is very important, dear apostles. Do not impose your leadership above the rightful leadership with the mistaken notion that you are in fact superior to the superior. This is an 'old faithful' for the devil. This is pride which always seeks to cross the bridges to places like superiority, jealousy, envy and lastly, to hatred. Do not let your issues contaminate your role in God's formation of our young people. Love, love and then add another bit of love. That will usually be the best way to encourage our youth. And we must all assume that we are being asked by God to encourage any young Christians we encounter.

Remember that young people are basing their beliefs on something. We will not know what these beliefs are based upon unless we are willing to listen, at length. One young man was accused of being an atheist. He was known as an atheist. Upon examination, he discovered he was not an atheist, but against all organized religion. Upon further examination, he discovered he was not against all organized religion, but against hypocrisy. This occurred because he had experienced cruel hypocrisy. He made the common mistake of attributing the characteristics of a Pharisee to the whole Church. He was repelled by these inconsistencies. This made him exactly like Jesus Christ. The young man discovered all of this by himself because someone listened attentively as he verbally worked it out.

What was the contribution of the apostle? Compassionate listening. Did the young man need counseling? Lecturing? Superiority? Disdain? No. He needed to examine his wound and see that it had dragged him to a faulty conclusion. His intelligence had brought him to a correct conclusion in the sense of a sum total that said, "This cruel judgment cannot be the product of a good God." But the equation was a little more complicated. Our young people are more than willing to accept flaws in older people if older people are willing to admit to these flaws. Generally speaking, young people are merciful and compassionate in the extreme.

May God give us all a willingness to self-examine before our death so that we can be used to best advantage on earth.

Part Seven

Questions and Answers

November 25, 2007

How does the Church lead with regard to non-Christians?

The Church leads first and always, through love. We must communicate love and respect to our non-Christian brothers and sisters. If they hold ill will toward us, we must openly acknowledge this, being clear to state that while we are wished ill, we hold only good wishes for our brothers and sisters in non-Christian faiths. It is important that we openly express our sadness and pain at such ill will, proclaiming our intention to pray for them and for peace between us.

Many of God's children have separated themselves from the Source of grace. They consequently experience fear and anxiety. How can we comfort them and draw them back into the safety of the Church without minimizing the reality of their sinful condition?

The reality of their condition is no match for the inexhaustible quantity of God's mercy. All discussions about God's mercy should remain separate from discussions about the consequences of their sin. When God's mercy is being discussed, God's mercy should be allowed to stand alone as a remedy for this time. When, on the other hand, sin is being discussed, one should always point first to the effect of the sin on the individual, the sinner, because this is where sin damages first. Only after this discussion should one move into the impact of the sin on others. Sin first wounds the soul of the sinner and creates sadness and grief. Next, sin moves with great determination out into the world around the sinner. Heaven mitigates fiercely when invited to do so. God's mercy is the balm that should be carried out to those who have drifted away from the Church. Press God's mercy into the world and sinners will return.

Yes, God's mercy is the remedy for all fear and anxiety. The truth, when accompanied by God's mercy, is both instructive and consoling. Each soul carries within it the seed of goodness planted by the Father. It is often God's mercy that germinates the seed, which then identifies the truth. Far from causing further anxiety, this germination, initiated by mercy, readies the soul for acceptance of all truth, but most particularly those truths that relate to the condition of the individual.

The answer to the following question is both evident and elusive. Men ponder it for years.

Why does God require man's participation in the redemptive act?

Jesus died, as we know, to free us from our sins. When Jesus accepted the cross, He accepted it on behalf of and in union with all men of good will. The fact that God allows us to participate in the redemption of our brothers and sisters is further proof of His great benevolence and further proof of His determination that we become part of His family, instead of remaining outsiders.

Each life contains suffering. The plan for each individual includes the experience of suffering in order to allow the individual to participate in the redemptive act. When a person seeks to avoid suffering to the degree that he departs from the will of God, he is refusing to participate in God's plan for him and for the greater family. He is refusing his determined share of the redemptive act. Often, suffering comes from those around us. Our duty to these people ensures that we are allowed a portion of the cross.

Suffering is always accompanied by grace. The greater the suffering, the greater the amount of grace that is made available by heaven. Will the individual accept the grace? That is a matter for the individual to decide.

It should never be forgotten that Jesus Christ felt abandoned on Calvary. That was part of the redemptive act and this experience is part of the participation in the redemptive act for many. The example set by the Lord in His Passion illustrates the plan that the Father has for every person in their participation in the redemptive act.

And so it is true that what God requires from us and what God allows for us are two very different matters. You could say that God does not require the participation of humanity at all. You could say that God does not need us. And yet, does any Father need his child when the child is an infant? Is it not more accurate to say that the infant needs the Father more than the Father needs the infant? Despite this, the Father experiences joy through His infant and then, by accepting the nourishment provided by the Father, the infant grows and develops. Later, through a decision made in free will, the child begins to assist the Father and help with the Father's interests and it is in this movement to freely-willed service that the Father experiences additional joy in the child and the child experiences security in the family of the Father.

How does the experience of eternity differ between those of one faith and those of another?

This is an excellent question and the answer is simple. Eternity differs from one person to the next in that each individual rests in the truths of eternity differently, according to his experiences and his desire for truth.

The desire for truth is divinely placed in each soul but

many reject the call to seek God during their time on earth.

With regard to faiths, God has placed the greatest amount of truth available to humanity within the Catholic Church. God continues to reveal His presence and His truths within the Catholic Church. The Catholic Church is the protector and defender of God's truth on earth.

This is not to say that God does not reveal Himself to those in other faiths. This is not to say that at all. Each man who seeks God will find Him because the search for the divine is a common thread which binds all men together. God will never disappoint a desire to find Him.

Other faiths contain God's truth to a greater or lesser extent. Those called to Catholicism have an obligation to preach the Gospel message according to the faith of their Church, which has been protected and defended through the years. It is only in the pure representation of the message that others will be attracted to the Church. Any dilution of God's truth will result in a less potent and less compelling call.

God is good. This is a perfect truth and many faiths accept this as a perfect truth. However, the extent of God's goodness can only be explored fully in eternity and all of eternity will be necessary to absorb the extent of His goodness. That is one example of a true statement illustrating but the barest extent of a majestic and limitless reality.

All men were created to spend eternity with the Father. God's love for each person is unique and irreplaceable. To say that God would welcome one child home and deny another is to negate His perfect goodness. Beware of any faith that promotes such thinking. The truths of God's Kingdom are available for study on earth, however, and those who complete these studies on earth, through the teachings placed in the one true Church, will move swiftly into the mysteries of the Kingdom in eternity.

Some men, in their humanity, seek to place themselves above others. This is the opposite of heavenly teaching. God loves all men equally. And yet it should not be denied that God's plan includes an apostolic tradition that is both willed and protected by heaven.

How does the Church respond to those who say we are arrogant in our claim of holding the deposit of faith?

In the Lord's time, He was called arrogant for claiming heavenly Kingship. If the Lord had denied His Kingship, they would have spared His life, but to do so would have required the Lord to deny the truth. He chose to die for the truth of His Father's Kingdom. Was the Lord arrogant? No. He proclaimed the truth with perfect humility.

Are we, the Church, arrogant to claim a truth which was purchased for us through the King's blood? No. We must respond as the Lord did, humbly defending the truth of the Kingdom of God. Our call is made more compelling by the fact that it is not only our truth we are defending, but the truth that justly belongs to each man, regardless of his faith.

Just as Jesus died willingly for the very souls who condemned Him, we must accept all suffering for the very ones who seek to destroy God's Church.

How should the Church seek reconciliation with those faiths that have fallen away?

The Church should maintain a position of guardianship of God's truth by returning to a pure representation of that which has been placed within her.

What is the nature of the Trinity?

The nature of the Trinity is love. Each person of the Trinity possesses the fullness of love, which flows constantly through each person to the other persons of the Trinity. This love is a moving, living, encompassing reality which is, by its definition, invitational. It draws and pulls. People can best understand the nature of the Trinity by considering their feelings toward a person who is completely innocent and completely lovable, as in an infant who is a member of that person's family. The nature of the love felt for one such as this is protective, and also fills with delight. God, in the three persons of the Trinity, feels this way toward each man.

Why is God so misunderstood by humanity?

God is not misunderstood by humanity. It is more accurate to say that God is *rejected* by humanity. Those who seek to reject God participate in an active, ongoing rejection because to cease rejecting means to participate in conversion. Those who reject God seek not clarity, but ambiguity, which is then offered as a means of bolstering their decision for rejection. If one admits to the barest understanding of God, one who rejects Him must admit to willfully choosing self over God. It is less damning to claim that one rejects a false version of God than to honestly admit to rejecting goodness. The action of rejecting God always leads to sin.

Why does heaven deprive humanity of the divine vision during their time on earth?

Heaven dulls the mystical senses so that humanity can choose God freely. The Kingdom of heaven is present on earth in each man of good will who welcomes the Spirit. God intends that the Kingdom be both present and spread through His existence in the souls of the just, who represent all of the members of the family of God in their decision to follow the Master. If the mystical senses were completely available to men during their time on earth, there would be no choice to make, no struggle to overcome, no share in the redemptive act. Heaven would then be filled with those who simply went with the flow of the stream, as opposed to making a choice for goodness through a rejection of evil.

There would be self in the decision for heaven, as opposed to selflessness.

Heaven is love and the heavenly Kingdom is filled with love and those who reside in heaven love seamlessly. There can be no lukewarm commitments in heaven because each individual in heaven is perfectly committed to every other member of the family of God.

Man is denied full access to the divine vision on earth so that man can examine both good and evil and ultimately, through cooperation with grace, choose good freely.

Why does one person receive greater or lesser mystical gifts than another during their time on earth?

Each person is given exactly what he or she requires to fulfill God's intended plan of service for Him. No two mystical experiences on earth are alike as no two people are alike.

One man is given few exceptional mystical experiences, yet he serves consistently, making choice after choice for the family of God and God's Kingdom. Toward the end of his life, he experiences great doubts, forcing him to closely examine his choices and decisions in life. In looking at God through what he knows of Him as expressed in his faith, and by faith

I mean his Church, he decides that righteousness is preferable to evil and truth preferable to deception. He chooses God again, even in his lack of certainty. He then begins to serve in a more determined fashion because he has made a decision to stand with a God he cannot see or touch. His living of his decision gives him the greatest glory. His act of commitment is heroic, given his struggle with doubt, and when he finishes his time on earth and comes to God, he is welcomed accordingly.

Isn't it true that he was given exactly what he needed to become a great saint?

Another man is given many mystical gifts and experiences. He struggles, however, with the pull of the world and makes only half-hearted commitments to service. The gifts in his soul sit on a back shelf, unused. It must be understood that he will be asked to account for every gift that he has been allowed. His decision to serve in lukewarm fashion or not at all will be examined in the light of the exceptional graces he has been allowed. Toward the end of his life, he is drawn even more to the world and, rather than evaluate what he knows and choose complete service, the service that has been intended for him, he wastes his time and exults in the offerings of the world. Did the mystical gifts guarantee him great holiness? No. On the contrary, in this case these gifts will stand as further testament against him when he examines his life with Jesus in truth.

All people receive exactly the gifts required to serve in the manner intended for them. One person would have no use for the mystical gifts of another.

Why does science seem to deny the existence of God?

True science cannot and does not deny the existence of

God. How could it? Rather, it is erroneous and limited scientific thinking that is used in an attempt to deny the existence of God. In this time, as in no other time, science has become arrogant. If there is humility in science, God's truth is further illuminated for man. An arrogant approach to science can be thought of as mankind attempting to kick down doors that have been locked against them. The door will never be opened in this way. The scientist will only wound himself and others in the process of trying to gain illicit access. In God's good time, He opens doors to humble scientists and invites them to walk through. One can identify what is true and what is erroneous by simply identifying what gives glory to God and what seeks to discredit the existence and dominion of God.

Part Eight

Homosexuality

Homosexuality

By active homosexuality we refer to sexual relationships between men or between women. How difficult it must be to discover this orientation for a Catholic who checks and confirms that *yes, this is really how I feel.* How confusing, given that his or her faith teaches against these practices. In order to satisfy these urges, one would be compelled to act against our faith, which might leave one feeling guilty, or perhaps defiant and angry.

Possibly heterosexuals could compare this to the feelings experienced in situations of pre-marital sex or extra-marital sex or even sex after a divorce situation without an annulment and remarriage. The parameters are clear. Holy behavior does not include these things. And yet many fail.

Possibly at this time, more fail than succeed, at least initially. Certainly, many people who fail experience at least a fleeting frustration with God's call to chastity. Many people find themselves in extremely difficult situations and when examining Church teaching they can feel overwhelmed by the call to chastity. Also, it is a tough thing to examine one's life in any of the above situations, homosexual and heterosexual, and observe that a holy future does not appear to include sexual intercourse, which society is telling us is necessary for happiness.

Yes, at least initially, this could feel overwhelming.

I am thinking of a child looking into an impossibly messy bedroom after being told to clean it. How many children, and we are all children in the eyes of God, feel overwhelmed and powerless to meet the request? A child would be tempted to sit down on the floor and cry over the impossibility of his circumstances. Maybe to add to his distress, there is something that appears to be an immovable object in the middle of the room. He has tried to move it but it won't budge. The child thinks, 'I would have enough trouble handling the rest of the mess but with this immovable object, I am certain of failure. What is the point of trying?' He gives up.

Perhaps then the child is forced to watch other children, who do not have these seemingly immovable objects, move past him with airs of superiority because their rooms appear cleaner. Clearly, these other children would not be exhibiting superiority if they were doing real work in their own rooms and if one looks under their beds one is often unpleasantly surprised.

Anyway, perhaps another sibling comes by and looks at the immovable object with this child. Perhaps he also studies it. Perhaps what this sibling does is sit with his brother and keep him company, encouraging him to wait until the father comes to deal with the object. And the father will come. Fathers always do. And what is impossible for a child is easy work to a father.

In truth, nobody should be asked to take on a task that is too big and too difficult by himself. In the faith life, nobody is. The room that is our soul is perfected not in an instant but over time. And what is impossible for us by ourselves is possible for us with the help of God. God is not discouraged regardless of the condition of our rooms. I think the Lord would advise this child to see to other areas in the room while praying and waiting for help to come.

In what form will God send help? This is hard to know. God is multi-talented in terms of creatively approaching our obstacles. He might send help in the form of other siblings who can assist in carrying the weight of the object. He might help the child to dismantle it and move it out little by little over time. Or He might simply move the thing Himself. One thing is for sure. The child will benefit from both studying this object and struggling with this object. It can be no other way. God allowed the object to be there and, if allowed, God will ultimately use the situation for the benefit of the child himself and all of humanity.

What would the Lord say to the brothers and sisters of this child? I think He would tell them to be available to assist their sibling if asked. I am certain He would tell them to rejoice in the presence of these brothers and sisters in their lives and to love them constantly and completely, as He loves them. He would encourage each to pray for the other and He would hope that all would both give mercy to each other and be open to receiving mercy from each other. In short, get on with the relationships in love whenever possible because we need each other.

Struggling with any obstacle can bring a person to wonderful humility and compassion and this world is in need of both of these things.

Additionally, I believe God would ask those who experience physical attraction to people of their own gender to return love for hostility, as He Himself did. Jesus was mistreated, misjudged, and misunderstood. He was maligned, slandered, and ultimately condemned. Through it all, He spread the Father's love. Now if these types of unfair treatments describe our experience in any way, then we can be sure that Jesus is nodding His head and saying, *"I certainly remember that feeling."* Poor Jesus was blameless. We, in our humanity, are never entirely blameless but if we suffer as Jesus suffered, we should beg Him for the grace to allow our suffering to bring us to holiness, never bitterness.

Would Jesus tell any of us to go against our Church's teaching? No. Even while God's love is unconditional and therefore constant, unaffected by our sins or rebellion, I believe He hopes we will eventually defer to Him and to His teaching in our Church, even if this is done in baby steps.

The Catechism treats this subject and all matters of sexuality with truth, calling on humanity to reserve the use of the sexual faculty for marriage. In other words, we all depart from God's plan if we use our sexual faculty outside of a sacramental marriage union.

For clarification, it is important to note here that the Church recognizes lust, masturbation, fornication, pornography, prostitution and rape also as departures from chastity. It would be a good exercise for everyone to look for themselves on this list before judging anyone else.

This writing in no way seeks to beat anyone over the head with their sexual departures from holiness. God Himself knows there has been enough of that to last us all well into forever, but there is a commonality to the call to chastity that cannot be denied by either heterosexuals or homosexuals.

What does the Church teach about chastity? The Catechism states that chastity includes an "apprenticeship in self-mastery" (2339). These words console. They do not say, "Be chaste immediately or give up, cast yourself out of the family and be damned." This is not what these words say. The word apprenticeship implies learning. Learning involves process. We are all called to be constantly involved in a process that moves us toward chastity.

We may say, "It is too hard. I cannot do it. I will never succeed."

But most people initially feel this way when they begin to work on a virtue. If we turn away, giving up, what we are really saying is, "I do not want this virtue."

This is fair enough. Our free will allows for this, but we must be honest and admit that we are refusing to try rather than make a claim that God has made it impossible for us to succeed.

Who is to judge success? Only God is the legitimate judge of success and failure with regard to humanity and our struggle with any of the virtues. There is a reason for the Sacrament of Confession. God's expectations are realistic. He expects us to struggle at times, meaning, to be perfectly clear, He knows that we will sin and He also hopes that we will repent. Even the greatest saints sinned, repented, then tried again. There is a massive, well-documented precedent for struggle in the Christian walk. We may think of Mary Magdalene perhaps, or even St. Paul who stated:

7 In view of the extraordinary nature of these revelations, to stop me from getting too proud I was given a thorn in the flesh, an angel of Satan to beat me and stop me from getting too proud!

8 About this thing, I have pleaded with the Lord three times for it to leave me, but he has said, 'My grace is enough for you; my power is at its best in weakness.' So I shall be very happy to make my weaknesses my special boast so that the power of Christ may stay over me, and that is why I am quite content with my weaknesses, and with insults, hardships, persecutions, and the agonies I go through for Christ's sake. For it is when I am weak that I am strong (2 Cor 12).

Perhaps we can remember someone known for being impatient and cantankerous. Perhaps that person spent his or her whole life insulting others and snapping back at those around him. To an outsider, it might look like this person failed to master the virtue of charity and perhaps this is true. But could any of us reject as hopeless the idea that at the time of his or her death the Lord looked kindly on the terrible battle of the individual? Would any of us dare to say that God would reject that person's efforts because we, in our pitifully limited human knowledge, failed to personally observe repentance and understanding? Do any of us really know the struggle endured by that person? That person's beliefs? Understanding? Formation?

Additionally, it is possible that this same person excelled in other areas which we know nothing about. Only God knows the full truth which is why, happily for us all, only God will judge.

The Catechism further notes that man either governs his passions or becomes dominated by them, causing unhappiness (2339).

Who can deny that the call to govern our passions is shared by all mankind? When man fails to govern his passions, we have serious consequences quickly. To argue that man should be encouraged to give way to his sexual passions is to argue for hell on earth because not all passions are good or appropriately actionable. It should not alarm us that some of our desires are bad desires, not rooted in God's plan. Indeed, we should expect this to be the case.

Additionally, overcoming ourselves and gaining mastery over ourselves must be viewed as a lifetime project. At various times we will struggle with temptations against chastity, usually more at sometime in our life than at other times. But we must all be aware that temptations can sneak up on us even long after we think we have conquered them.

Since chastity is a gift from God, a grace, a fruit of spiritual effort, we must ask for it. We must tell God often that we recognize chastity as something valuable and that we desire to possess it. God is so good. He wants this for us but He wants us to participate in the acquisition of the virtues through willingness and effort. Like all things of value, chastity is worth striving for and protecting.

There is a contention amidst modern society that anything is acceptable in sexual matters as long as it is being done by consenting adults. This contention is problematic. How does mutual consent diminish sin? The fact that we can gain the participation and camaraderie of another does not mean the actions we commit together are good. Departures from holiness are departures from holiness regardless of how many people commit them, condone them or claim to enjoy them.

In this time, there is the idea that every person should have what he chooses, when he chooses and with whomever he chooses. But truly and honestly, when was this ever acceptable? When will it ever become acceptable? It is not heaven's job to adapt itself to our physical desires. These desires are unbelievably temporary and changeable when compared to eternity. It is rather our job to gradually, perhaps over our lifetime, adapt ourselves to heaven's permanent state of purity.

Nobody should look at sexual desires that prompt a departure from holiness and be tricked into believing that they were created to behave in this manner. This would be like God setting us up for failure. The idea flies completely in the face of His nature. We were all created to become pure.

There is a temptation for some to define themselves by their sexual urges. At this time, a whole identity has been created to match the urges. This, while understandable, seems cruelly limiting and I believe further takes our brothers and sisters away from us and us from them. There is responsibility on both sides of the fence for this division and as such both sides are ultimately called to repair this division with love. Judgments against either side, by either side, should be avoided.

With regard to the identity, however, it must be argued that for Catholics this is the same as accepting any other kind of action against chastity and not only claiming helplessness but actually identifying oneself by the temptation. This could lead further and further into defiance and away from Jesus.

In other times in history, it seems that it was readily accepted that not every person was intended for marriage or for marital intimacy and by this I do not refer simply to the act of sexual intercourse but also all that comes with marriage, which is, it must be said, a considerable package of sacrifice.

Perhaps we need to examine the misunderstood concept of intimacy.

Those who remain single or choose either a chaste or celibate lifestyle are not prohibited from intimacy. On the contrary, there are many kinds of intimacy and all of humanity is designed to experience some kind of intimacy.

From heaven's perspective, what is intimacy? As previously stated, intimacy takes place when two souls meet to the accompaniment of a special grace. I believe this takes place in the divine will, in other words, in the Lord's company which means in love because intimacy is really a cloudburst of love. Intimacy is the communication of love. Grace creates an opening, an opportunity, and a pure exchange can then take place.

How does this occur? What actually happens?

Well, it depends. It can occur with words or with silence. It can be limited to a gaze that holds steady, a momentary glance, or even a small physical touch. We will know when we have experienced real intimacy because something goes out and something comes back. There is an exchange.

Another sign of intimacy is that both people are affected in some way. They experience things like encouragement that strengthens them or companionship that lessens terrible loneliness. Both know that they are loved. Maybe one is simply informed through this experience of intimacy that there is someone else in the world who accepts him and desires to understand him, even if he does not understand him or cannot understand him. The desire, the good will is enough to lessen the pain of isolation.

This pure intimacy or true intimacy is available to all men and women since it is really just the communication of love which is not limited and cannot be limited to genders or between genders. It has nothing to do with genders and is unrelated to physical sexual expression even while it can be available in the act of sexual expression. It is for this reason that it is short-sighted, and I would guess terribly hurtful, to deny that there can be authentic love between those who are involved with homosexuality. Who can say that? Who would dare make such a judgment? No one can know what happens between two people with regard to real intimacy.

If Jesus limited pure intimacy to those who were living perfectly according to our Church's teaching, there would be no hope of comfort in the world or indeed conversion because conversion is sparked by love and presupposes sinfulness and the need for change.

Why would we attempt evangelization? Without pure love evangelization would be impossible because people are drawn by pure love which can only be communicated through the intimacy I am pitifully attempting to describe. God gives grace wherever He chooses.

If we have decided that any group is incapable of heavenly expressions of love until they are perfect, then we must get comfortable being close to them because we are all in that same sad and helpless basket.

There are many in this time experiencing plenty of physical sexual activity but no pure intimacy. Conversely, there are many happy souls who experience plenty of intimacy with absolutely no physical sexual expression. One does not necessarily flow from the other.

The best writings on love I have ever read were written by a celibate man. I am referring to *God is Love*, the encyclical written by the Holy Father, Pope Benedict XVI.

We were all created to be heaven bound. I believe that most of us will, even if it is at the last possible moment, choose heaven over hell, Jesus over Satan.

At that time, what we will be choosing is an eternity made up of beautiful binding intimacy which will perfect our understanding of each other and complete our joy in each other.

We must be courageous in our search for purity and remember that we are all searchers. In heaven we will look at each other and rejoice in each other's goodness. We will take absolute delight in each other's uniqueness. Before then, we are called to cherish each other, even in our collective human state of imperfection.

Part Nine

Heaven Speaks

A Second Collection of Messages
to Specific Groups of Souls

Heaven Speaks to Those
Away from the Church

Jesus

December 9, 2006

I call out to those who have left My Church. Come back, I say. Return to the safety of the sacramental walk. It will be best for you and I want only what is best for you. Be assured of My welcome. Be assured that I want your return. Do not think that you are unwelcome in your faith. How could this be when I, Jesus Christ, personally call out to you? My Church on earth represents Me. It is My Church and belongs to Me. When the people of My Church accurately represent Me, you feel cherished. I want to restore you to your Church and I want to restore your Church to you. You see, My friend, it is best for you, given your call to holiness, that you proceed on the path that is protected by My Church on earth. I have so many ways to help you if you are following your faith within the protection of My Church. My Church has suffered, it is true. My Church continues to suffer. Part of the reason My Church is suffering is because you are away from it. My Church needs you. My Church wants you. You must return.

Beloved child, I am asking you, indeed, I am pleading with you to consider your circumstances. If there are reasons that inhibit a full return to the sacraments for you, I ask that you discuss these reasons with one of My priests. I will protect your desire to return to the sacraments. I will not reduce the standards of My Church for your circumstances, but I will help you to adapt your circumstances to those standards. "What is Jesus saying?" you ask yourself. Let Me be more clear. This time on earth is a time when so many have compromised with standards of behavior that the compromised standards have become the norm. I cannot and will not accept this. I do not accept this. If I were to accept this, I would have to change all of heaven and all of those who have served in times before you. Also, I would have to jeopardize the future of all those who come after you. My friend, listen to Me. Hear My words because My words are truth. Reject the rebelliousness of My enemy. Accept that you are called to follow Me and raise your behavior to My standards. I will help you. You will be welcome in heaven if you accept that I am God. You will have to accept that I am God in order to gain heaven, of course. Will you not accept this fact now, before your time on earth is finished? Will you return to Me now, given that ultimately you hope to do so? My heart longs for your peace. I see everything. If you have been hurt by those who claimed to represent My Church but who failed, I will heal you. Do not use this hurt as a reason why you step away from all that I offer for you through My Church. This has taken you in the wrong direction and others walk behind you. Please, come into My Church. It belongs to Me, after all. You are welcome, regardless of your sins.

St. Monica

December 11, 2006

I send my greetings to all of God's children. I speak today particularly to those who are Catholics but who are living away from their faith. You are invited by heaven to return to your faith. Heaven, God and all of the saints, urges you to consider returning to the sacraments. If you have been away from the Church for some time, you may want to have your Confession heard. This is a good place to start. Talk to a priest about this because graces are waiting for you in this sacrament. With these graces you can examine your life and determine how to proceed on a new path, a path that leads back to Jesus through the Church. You may reject this concept. You may reject the Church as the best route to Jesus Christ. My friend, that is your choice but do not be confused. We are trying to protect you. The words and graces in this work are a gift to you, personally. If you choose not to accept this gift, that is your decision. I want you to accept the gift of these graces because with them you will find greater peace. Jesus loves you. You know this. God accepts you. You must believe this. If you do not return to God's Church on earth, you will still be loved and accepted, given the proper spirit of repentance in your soul. We want more for you, though, and we need more from you. If you return to the Church, we can restore you to unity with the Communion of Saints working for the salvation of many at this time. You will be drawn into the mission of renewal and this benefits you and all of those people around you. I ask you to do something for me. Come to a church and sit in silence in front of the tabernacle. Jesus is there. Sit in silence and ask Jesus what He wants you to do. Do not be angry at Jesus for the sins of mankind. Do not blame Jesus for the mistakes of mankind. Jesus is trying to help you. You belong in His Church and His Church needs you. Bring any anger to Jesus and explain to Him what happened to make you feel that you should walk away from your Church.

Perhaps you have simply drifted. Please, drift back now. Come and sit with Jesus and talk to Him about your life. What are your worries? What are your joys? Tell Jesus about these things. Share these things with Jesus. You will find a welcome, I assure you. Jesus welcomes you and your family welcomes you. You belong in this Church and your home is in this Church. We will all help you.

St. Monica

Dear friend of heaven, there is great confusion in your world. The enemy of God, your enemy, seeks to divert attention away from the truth. To do this, satan has placed noise everywhere. How often do you work in silence? How often do you sit in silence and simply rest? God's poor little children are so distracted and over-stimulated that they do not feel comfortable in quiet. Their minds and hearts cannot rest. This situation is unacceptable and it is for this reason that so many in the world feel agitated and unhappy. They are no longer comfortable in quietness. They do not understand how to feed themselves spiritually. Because of this they hunger, but they know not for what. God's children, and I am speaking of adults, say that they are bored in Mass. Dear friend of heaven, you are not paying attention if you are bored. Seek Jesus and you will not be bored. Jesus will always be found by those who seek Him. Those who do not seek Him could bump into Him and they would not recognize Him. I am sad about this state of affairs. I love Jesus and I know that Jesus is the answer for the pain of mankind, but there are so few who are willing to fight for their Savior. Think about your brothers and sisters in the world who have lived in the pain of isolation from heaven. *Many have left this life unprepared for heaven because of the constant noise and distraction in their life. Stand with God, my friend. Take up your share of the weight of His cross and advance God's army as far as He wills for you. This is not a time to be superior to Jesus Christ and His Church. This superiority will end abruptly when you die and face Him. End it now. Do not be cynical about your Church. Return to your Church and walk into the mystery of your faith. Jesus will reveal Himself and heal all of your wounds if you do this. Your sins will be forgiven, of course, and the Church will help you to find your way to unity with the Body of Christ. I urge you to come back to your family. Please. We need your help.*

St. Monica

Turn your eyes to heaven, my friend. Look up. If you look up to heaven and rest in heaven's truths, you will not be as concerned with the mistakes made by humanity in God's Church. You will walk toward heaven in unison with those who have been called to allow the renewal to flow through them. You live in a time when Jesus returns to the world. This is the time of the Advent of the Second Coming. The triumphant return of Jesus Christ is a core belief for the faithful. It is nothing to argue about or attempt to refute. I am telling you today that the Lord has begun to return through all who welcome Him in their soul. If you are a Catholic, you can be most effective by serving from within the Church. If you return to the Church, God can fill you until His graces overflow. This overflow pushes out into the world, spreading light in place of darkness and truth in place of error. This is the plan, my friend. This is the renewal. The return of Jesus Christ today hinges upon your willingness to become holier. The return of Jesus Christ today hinges upon your willingness to say "no" to selfishness and "yes" to Jesus. God is asking for your help. I, Monica, am asking for your help. You may come to Jesus and request an abundant amount of graces for your return to faithfulness. Jesus will give you these graces. Jesus wants you back in the Church and He will send all that is necessary to assist you in this return. The only thing Jesus cannot supply is your willingness. Willingness must come from you. Dear child of God, the world does not love you. We love you. The world cannot protect you. We can protect you. The world does not offer you eternal safety and joy. Only heaven can offer this to you. Make a decision for Jesus today, understanding that the decision you make for Jesus is really a decision for yourself and your loved ones. Jesus will never let you go if you come to Him, and through you He can begin to protect your family and loved ones. We, God's saints, will help you. Be brave and come back to your Church.

Blessed Mother

Welcome, my beloved child. I say welcome because I am anticipating your complete return to faithfulness. I know that your heart is open and it is for this reason that you have been given these words at this time. You feel a longing in your heart. My child, I am Mary, your heavenly mother. You long for truth and I bring you truth. Heaven is here. Heaven is filled with those who love you and seek your safety. Do not think that your sins are different from the sins of those who reside in heaven. Humanity struggles in predictable ways. Often the struggles of humanity are related to wounds inflicted by others who also struggle. We are called to forgive, of course, and this can be difficult. But you are one who seeks my Son so I will obtain for you an abundance of forgiveness. A mother's tender heart and sympathetic listening ear can soothe any bitterness. I am listening to you now, my little one. Tell me what hurts you. Tell me what has hurt you in the past. I will help you to heal and bring you back to Jesus in a spirit of newness. You see, the renewal of mankind is taking place one soul at a time. Today, I concern myself with the renewal in your soul. When we renew your soul, together, you and I will proceed to the place where Jesus needs you to serve the Kingdom. Often, this place of service is the place you are at right now. In other words, Jesus does not need you to do something different. He needs you to do the same things differently. Do you understand? Jesus wants you to serve in unity with Him and all of your brothers and sisters working for the renewal. You will serve in joy, not despair. You will serve in hope, not hopelessness. You will serve with the knowledge that you are making a difference to the world as you depart from the place of bitterness and hurt. At times, God's children have to move to another place of service. Regardless, they never proceed alone. I am your mother. You feel my presence, I know. Come into my arms and I will surround you with protection and grace while heaven renews your soul and brings you back to your Church.

Heaven Speaks to Those Considering Suicide

Jesus

November 29, 2006

I have many things to say to those who are considering this act of self-harm. I love you. I see your pain. I understand that you long for relief from your anguish. Please, bring your anguish to Me. I can help you. You are so valuable to the Kingdom and I need you to help bring Me to others.

"How?" you say, in your great interior grief. "How could I possibly be helpful to Jesus and to others?"

I will tell you. Your pain is the pain of many in the world today. Many souls feel your grief, your hopelessness. Many carry heavy crosses of illness and addiction, loneliness and hopelessness, rejection and anxiety. Many of My children look into their future and see only more grief and pain and this takes their courage from them. Dearest friend, you must not do this. Do not look into tomorrow and expect today's pain to be repeated. You are not certain of such an occurrence. You cannot be certain because I, God, could change your life during this day, today. You must remain in this day, in the present, because I have given you adequate grace to deal with your cross. It is only when you look into the future and think that your Jesus will send you no relief that you find life unmanageable. Understand this. Your life is only unmanageable if you put Me out of it. If you let Me into your heart, into your life, I will make it not only manageable, but joyful.

You are skeptical. You cannot believe in a future with joy because the present holds such pain. I understand this, just as I understand everything about you. You may not know Me well so I will tell you something about Myself that may help you to decide that trusting Me is a good decision.

I have never been known to break a promise. Never. Today, I have a promise for you.

If you ask Me to help you, I will help you. Ask Me, My beloved one. You are important to this Kingdom and I have a plan for you. I need you. I need you to serve in a way that you do not and cannot understand today, in your great hopelessness. I will reveal the plan but you will have to be courageous and allow Me to move you from this place of despair to a place of hope in your heart. I will do so. I will move you along, away from your sadness. You must trust Me just a little bit and give Me just a little bit of time. Even now, as you read these words, hope is stirring within you. This hope is from Me and it is the smallest indication of what I will bring to you. I am giving you courage. I am giving you hope. Rest with Me.

Say this, "I will rest myself against Jesus and wait for Him to send relief."

I will send relief. Do not be afraid. I am with you now and I will never leave you.

St. Margaret Mary Alacoque

November 30, 2006

Dear little soul, you are in pain. Your anguish feels deep, I know. Often, the most difficult part of suffering anguish is the perception that nobody understands the depth of your pain. One can feel very alone in such pain and when one seeks out consolation from others, one is often terribly disappointed. Please listen to me. I am your sister in Christ. I experienced great anguishes while I was on earth so I am rejoicing that God allows me to help you. When you go to another seeking comfort and you find yourself in worse shape, feeling even more misunderstood and alone, you must come to me. Say, "Margaret, I need help. I need help now."

I, Margaret, will go directly to the throne of God and I will remain there until you receive the comfort and courage you require. My friend, it is important that you know that you are not suffering alone. Jesus sees your suffering. He feels it with you and His Sacred Heart is moved to the most passionate desire to assist you. You must allow our Jesus to help you. When you make this emergency prayer to me, Margaret, you are really saying that you are willing to let heaven help you. How heaven rushes in at this time! You will know that I have heard you because you will feel a change. It may be just a whisper of a change, just a little shifting. It will be noticeable to you as a feeling of calm in your spirit. When you feel this little feeling of calm, you will know that you have been heard, that help is on the way and that you are not alone in your suffering. You have my promise that heaven will surround you until the frightening feelings pass.

I want to say something else. It is common for a person on earth to have thoughts that are not from God. Everyone on earth struggles with this at some time. We could say, actually, that everyone on earth struggles with this each day in terms of temptations. The battle is not finished until you die in your body and come to God's Kingdom. Given this, the constant need for struggle, you must view your thoughts of suicide as temptations. Do not be alarmed by these thoughts in that simply having these thoughts does not mean there is any reason to act on these thoughts. Do you understand? Do not be afraid. We, the saints in heaven, all had bad thoughts and temptations during our time on earth and we all at times failed to fight off temptations. The temptation to commit suicide is one where you must fight hard, with everything you have because of the nature of the consequence. If you take your life, you will not be able to go back and say, "Jesus, I want to do better and serve You now." You take away any second chances for yourself to convert to Jesus and try again. Dear friends, this is wrong for you. It is not the answer you are seeking.

Jesus needs you to stay in the world until it is the right time for you to come home. This is God's plan and it is always best to follow God's plan. The last day of your life is determined by God. You must not think that the answer to great pain is suicide. This act of self-harm is always a mistake. Always.

St. Margaret Mary Alacoque

My friend, you have been hurt. I see that. I understand that you are carrying wounds that cause you to ache. You may not even understand the source of your pain and your wounds. You know that you are not perfect and that you make mistakes. Jesus accepts this about you and loves you most tenderly regardless of your mistakes. I want you to consider that others also make mistakes. Others fail in love and in kindness. Others are imperfect as we were all imperfect on earth. The mistakes made by others can cause us the greatest pain. We can carry wounds with us without even being aware that we are doing so. These wounds then spread to other areas of our hearts and result in a general state of pain that is hard to come back from.

Jesus suffered terribly on earth. He also carried wounds. Jesus, in His most Sacred Heart, understands exactly how you came to be in such pain. He knows more about the source of your pain and hopelessness than you do. My beloved friend, I beg you now to turn to Jesus. He will heal you from wounds you do not even know you are carrying. You have felt loss in your life and there is emptiness. Jesus will fill you up again and restore you to a state of hope and joy that will flow out from you to others. I am telling you that your great pain will recede. When your great pain recedes and joy takes its place, you will be so kind to others because you will understand how they are hurting. You will look at another in anguish and your heart will be moved to the greatest pity for him. You will say, "I remember feeling that badly." Only one who has suffered such anguish can really understand it. Would you agree? Do you remember a time when you spoke to someone about something that he had also experienced and you felt understood? It will be this way with your great pain, also, and someone who feels hopeless will gain hope from you. If you take your life, you will not be around to help this person in the future.

I want you to know that Jesus, in His most Sacred Heart, feels your pain. Jesus suffered so that we could be forgiven. The fact that Jesus suffered willingly does not in any way take away from the fact that Jesus suffered terribly. Perhaps, my friend, you can look up to Jesus and tell Him that you, in your suffering, understand something about His suffering. If you do this, all of heaven will rejoice because you will be on your way to becoming a saint. Believe this, my friend, because it is truth. Many will share with Jesus in His joy. Many will even respect His cross. But few are there on earth who will carry the cross and turn their eyes to the Lord in love during their suffering, which is what Jesus did. Do this, beloved one, and heaven will lighten your cross and remove this pain more quickly than you expect.

St. Margaret Mary Alacoque

December 1, 2006

I feel such compassion for you, my friend. When you are carrying a heavy cross, it is difficult to see that it will end. Sometimes, you do not believe it will ever end. In terms of human power, maybe it is even impossible that your cross will end. But nothing is impossible for heaven. In heaven, you see, we live with miracles happening all around us. When you come to heaven you will understand what I mean. If your situation requires a miracle from heaven, you should ask for one. Miracles are not impossible when you keep company with saints. Saints, indeed, are all about obtaining miracles from God. God gives us these things, these miracles, because we suffered with Him while we were on earth. You will be a saint if you suffer with Jesus. And then you will be able to obtain powerful graces, also. You will say, "God, please help this person." God will do so when He sees that you are making the smallest effort to accept your suffering with Jesus. You have influence in your suffering. You have intercessory power, which means that if you ask for graces for another, God will grant them. This may be difficult for you to accept because you feel so sad or angry but I will use my influence to obtain graces for you to help you to understand. You will see that your suffering, your pain, is being used by heaven to help others. It will pass, my friend. You will feel better. I make this promise to you in the presence of Jesus Christ. He will keep this promise for us.

St. Margaret Mary Alacoque

I am going to give you some advice. I am one who suffered great anguish on earth, as I said, so I am a good one to help you. Remain very calm during this time of upset. Do not panic. Do not act in haste. Let us, your heavenly friends, calm your spirit. If you deal with your pain in quiet, with an attitude of calm, you will be less likely to make bad decisions that create even more pain. It is best, indeed, if you can delay important decisions until you feel better. Be wise about your suffering and allow yourself to be quiet. This is not a bad thing. Spending time in silence, reflecting, will not harm you. While you are remaining in quiet, ask Jesus constantly for help. Ask Him to remove your pain as soon as possible, and ask Him to help others who are suffering this pain. You are joined to heaven, remember, so there are many of us in heaven who understand that you are suffering and seek to help you. You are not alone. We will never abandon you in your anguish. Ask heaven to send you calming graces and heaven will do so. Remember that you are important and that we love you very much. Your mistakes do not affect our love for you because we made mistakes, too. Heaven is filled with saints who were great sinners on earth. We repented and God forgave us. Be at peace about your mistakes because the experience you gain from your mistakes helps you later. Do you understand? God has a plan for you. Taking your life is not part of that plan. You are surrounded by saints and you are surrounded by angels. You belong to our family and you will have all that you need.

Blessed Mother

My dear little child, how heavy is your heart. I see that you are suffering and feeling alone. Dear beloved one, you are not alone now and you will never be alone. Even as you read these words, heaven surrounds you. The angels pray constantly for your recovery, for a return to joy for you. You must believe that I tell you the truth today. I am Mary, your mother, and I can only seek what is good for you. I will seek what is good for you right now, before the throne of God, and ask the Father to send you heavenly gifts of courage and calm. You will move through this day that is already passing into the past and tomorrow will be better. Each day will move you closer to recovery. Do not think for a moment that God will leave you with pain that is unmanageable. God will not do this. Ask for help and you will receive it. I am here, with you now, and I will make sure that you receive all that you need to move past this period of anguish. Heaven does not will this for you. Heaven wills hope for you. Heavenly graces filled with hope flow into your soul now. Rest in God's grace and I will secure all that is necessary for you. I am your mother. I love you completely. I will help you. May I ask you to help me with something? I ask that you turn away from anything that is causing you this pain. Walk away from habits that bring darkness into your little soul. I will give you the light to understand what is creating such pain. You will not be left confused. Your cross will be lightened. You have my assurance of this. Be at peace today because, truly, heaven hears your prayer and moves to answer your prayer. You will see heaven helping you in many ways, my beloved child. You are not alone.

Heaven Speaks to Those Who Are Dying

Jesus

December 5, 2006

My beloved one, change is coming. You feel this. You are preparing to finish your time on earth and begin your time in eternity. That day, the day of your death, will be a joyful day because you will return to Me. Do you consider your death joyfully? Perhaps not. Perhaps you are afraid. Dear little child of God, I want to help you with any fears that take away from your peaceful consideration of the next life. You see, in our humanity we fear death and suffering. I understand this perfectly because I also experienced a dread of suffering. I did not fear death, though. I knew that death would bring liberation for Me in that I would be free of the constraints I experienced in My body. Dear beloved one, it will be a liberation for you, too. When your body ceases to live, your soul will become fully alive. There is nothing to frighten you. I will be there for you. I will take you to Me and comfort you. You will feel safer than you have ever felt on earth. Do you believe this? You should believe this, My friend, because it is the truth. Reject My enemy, once and for all, and rest in My heart while heaven prepares you to come home. I will remain with you constantly, helping you, consoling you, preparing you. At the end, you will feel My peace surround-

ing you. I will do this for you if you let Me. Right now, at this time, I continue to make ready your reward. You see, your reward is not final yet because you are still serving. Perhaps you are serving in illness, in weakness, or in sadness and grief. Offer it to Me. Offer it all to Me, your Jesus, and with it I will do the most magnificent things for others still serving on earth. I will take your little offerings and use them to console the Father, who is rejected by so many. Our Father is so good. You will understand His goodness more fully soon, when you come to Me. I promise you, little beloved one, that you will rejoice in any offerings, however small, you gave to our Father during this final time of service on earth. Be filled with joy. I am with you and will never leave you. In your precious little heart, take My hand in yours. I will hold you steadily, never letting go, during the time of transition between your life on earth and your life in eternity. I am with you in each moment.

St. John the Apostle

Greetings to you, my beloved family member. I am a quiet visitor in your soul. I am quiet because I am reverent in the face of your preparation. You see, the Lord has willed that you be given these words and graces to calm your fears. A steady stream of grace will flow into your soul at this time, preparing you to make the transition to the heavenly Kingdom. How blessed you are! How merciful is Jesus to make these words and graces available to you! I am not surprised that Jesus does this for you. I am a witness to the great love Jesus holds for you. Jesus loves you so much that He cannot wait to give you heavenly gifts. He is giving them to you now so that you will have a foretaste of your reward. When you die, you will come into the family of God. We love each other very much because we love God and join God in His love for each of our brothers and sisters. This love is different from love on earth. This love never fails. This love never weakens or alters. The love we feel for you and for each other is a reliable and continuous state of existence. We see each other as we were in our humanity, flawed, and this makes us even more tender in our love. You see, dear friend, the times we failed on earth helped us to become humble. There is no arrogance in heaven and you are coming to heaven. I am telling you that if you made mistakes and committed sins you are exactly like the rest of us. Confess your sins and allow Jesus to free you from the hold they have on your soul. Jesus forgives. Jesus forgets. You must accept His forgiveness and allow Him to grant you acceptance for yourself. Jesus can make all things new and He will make you new when you come to Him. Have no fear about your welcome. You will be welcomed by Jesus and by your whole family. I, John, am an expert on the love of Christ. I rested in the love Jesus had for me and I am asking you to do the same. Rest in the love Jesus has for you. Let it encircle you and penetrate you. You are cherished by Jesus Christ. He accepts you just as you are. Be at peace, my friend. Remain in heavenly quiet and allow Jesus to put the final touches on your soul.

St John the Apostle

My dear friend, how often have you known contentment? In your life on earth, how often have you sat in silence, thanking God for all of your blessings? Perhaps you are a wise person and you have done this each day. I am glad. Perhaps you have been busy and distracted and you have not done this enough. It is time to change. For a moment, thank God for all that He has allowed you to experience on earth. You have seen great goodness. Where have you seen goodness? Consider this question. Think back with me to the people you knew who were good. Why were they good? What was it that impressed you about them? You have also seen great evil. Offer God a brief prayer for those whom you witnessed working against goodness and then think no more about them. God will be merciful, particularly if you ask Him to be. Come back now to the examples of great goodness because it is in this goodness that I want you to rest yourself. You will always remember those who were better than you in terms of following God or following holy principles. Be at peace in this. It is not to torment you that I bring these things to your mind, but to console you. If you think back to the good people you have observed, you will be thinking forward to the good people you are about to meet. Heaven is filled with people who made decisions for God. Heaven is also filled with people who chose against God, but who repented, allowing God to purify them. What you will remember about a good person is this. That person made decisions based on love. That person overcame his own desires for the needs or desires of others. That person often took a harder road in order to do the right thing. You will recall that the decisions to do the right thing cost that person something. There was sacrifice. Rejoice with me, John, as you consider the heroic goodness of another. In doing so you are becoming acquainted with heavenly principles, even as you remain on earth. This is a good exercise for you because we will bring you to the heavenly Kingdom soon. Anything you need to be comfortable here will be given to you in terms of graces. I would like to see you at peace. I would like to see you accepting yourself as Jesus accepts you. Do you wish you had more to offer to Jesus? We all did and I mean that sincerely. Every one of us who considered our lives wished we had more to give, that we had been better, loved more completely and selflessly, served without interruption, and accepted the truth of God's presence. If you wish you had been better, you will fit right in with us in heaven. Be at peace. Contemplate the goodness you have seen and believe that Jesus accepts you just as you are right now.

St. John the Apostle

Dear friend, we, your heavenly companions, whisper into the ears of your soul during this time. We are helping you to leave this world and enter the next. We do this to assist you and we do this because it gives us joy to see that you are nearly finished with your earthly labors. We are happy for you. Any expectations you have of heaven and God's Kingdom are certainly underestimates because nothing can prepare you for the love of the Father and nothing can prepare you for the love of the family you are about to meet. We are all together in God's love and God's love unites us. This is the truth. Another part of the truth that will delight you is the personal, intimate love God has for you. You will experience this in Jesus Christ, our beloved Friend and Savior. I lived for love of Christ on *earth. In heaven, I live **because** of the love of Christ. How far short I fall when I begin to talk about the love of Jesus Christ. It is like trying to describe an ocean by indicating a small cup of water. Still, even though one is destined to fall short, one must begin. Jesus loves you so much that He lived each day for you, personally. The fact that He lived each day on earth for you personally in no way detracts from the fact that He lived each day for me personally. Because of the nature of God, God can be equally present to each man simultaneously. You will come to us and you will be with Jesus. You will never be separated from Him again. You will know perfect security, perfect acceptance, and perfect intimacy with Him in heaven. My friend, there are those who will choose eternal separation from our beloved Jesus but you will not do so. You will choose Jesus. Choose Him now so that He can shower you with mercy, thus preparing you for your homecoming. Confess your sins. Admit to your failures. If you do this now, grieve for your sins, you will have begun the process of self-acceptance. Jesus forgives you if you repent. This is always the case. But you have the need in your humanity to accept yourself and become peaceful about your past sins. If you do this on earth, there will be no barrier to an immediate unity with Jesus, in other words, heaven. If you do not finish the work on earth, you will have a need to finish the work in the heavenly Kingdom, that is, in purgatory. I, John, am encouraging you to at least begin this process now. Either way, Jesus is all mercy, all forgiveness. If you trust in Jesus, in His mercy, He will reward you with an unlimited amount of this mercy. Oh, my dear friend, take my words to your heart and believe them. I am trying to help you by giving you good advice and accurate information. Be humble and accept me as your brother, who gives wise counsel. I am praying for you now. Ask me to help you in this process and I will do so. Peace be with you and with all those around you.*

Blessed Mother

My little child, how joyful I am to be with you. My heart rests with you as you contemplate God's mercy. There will be no difficulty with Jesus accepting you. If you feel the smallest desire to be with Jesus, to rest in His merciful gaze, you will do so. You belong to heaven, little child. Be very humble about your entrance into eternity. A good child, a faithful servant, comes to the door in humility. This is what you must do. God is great, very great. God is all goodness, all power. Comparatively, what are you? I will tell you. You are God's beloved and immeasurably cherished child. You are like a small infant in my arms, in need of comfort and nourishment. Allow yourself to be a small and helpless infant and I, your heavenly mother, will give you all that you need to appear before God. I know about God, my child, and I know about you. I know about heaven and I know about the family who prepares to welcome you. I know what you will need to be comfortable. Allow me to help you become comfortable. We are all here for you. We desire to make you comfortable. If you have a thought that troubles you, simply give it to me. I will see to it by either removing the thought from you or revealing God's truth about the matter. You will have peace. We, your heavenly family, surround you. We help to remove any bitterness that remains with you. I love you, my little child. You are dear to me. A mother does not leave her child when her child needs her and I will not leave you.

Heaven Speaks to Those
Who Do Not Know Jesus

Jesus

December 21, 2006

I am Jesus. I am God. I am complete in Myself. I am present in your world and I am present in heaven. You see, I am omnipresent. Even if you wish to, you cannot remove yourself from My presence on earth. I created earth. You might say the earth belongs to Me. All on it are also My creation. You, dear beloved one, were created by Me. Do I say that you belong to Me? I say it in another way. I say, I WANT you to belong to Me. I want to possess your heart. Why do I use the word heart when truly it is your soul that I seek? I use the word heart because people characterize the heart as the place where people hold the love they possess. If you have love, people say you have it in your heart. The heart is known as the source of love and the receptacle of love, so I, Jesus, tell you that I want to possess your heart. When it is all simplified, as it should be, I am saying that I want you to love Me. I love you. There is no problem there. I love you today and I will always love you. A difficulty we have is that you do not know Me. The only way for Me to teach you to love Me is for Me to reveal Myself to you, to allow you to know Me. For that reason I come to you today. I reveal Myself to you through these words

*and through the graces attached to them. If you
read these words and sit in silence, you will begin
to know Me. If you begin to know Me, truly, you will
begin to love Me. Forget anything that tempts you
to move away from these words and graces. Rest.
Be with Me. Allow Me to teach you about Myself.*

Jesus

*In your world today, there are many claims of
goodness. Some of these claims are true. Some of
these claims are false. I, Jesus, am not present in
lies. I do not rest in falseness. Truth has a pure
feel to it and truth does not change. If you want
to find truth, look back over time and see what
claims of truth have persevered. What are the
things that were true two thousand years ago?
You will find them if you look to see what has persevered through the ages. Two thousand years
ago, it was true that I came to bring salvation.
Today, that is still true. I came then and I come
today. I come for your salvation. I come so that
you will be saved. I come so that where there is
falseness, where you are being deceived, I will be
present with My truth.*

*Two thousand years ago, there was evil in the
world. Today, evil persists alongside good. Does
this mean evil is good? Has truth changed? No.
Just as truth never changes, so evil does not*

change. Evil simply changes its disguise. I, God, have not changed My character. When you first know someone, you know a few things about him. As you get to know someone better, you learn more. Over time and with consistent interaction, you begin to know someone well and you can then say that you understand that person.

I want you to understand Me. I am truth. To know Me, Jesus, you will have to know what is true and what is false. I will teach you this but it is not something that I can teach you all at once. Truth, in its great depth, must be absorbed gradually. For this reason I invite you to keep company with Me. If you do, I will teach you all you need to know to distinguish between the truth in your world and the deceit in your world. I will teach you to separate good from evil at a glance. I am the great Teacher, the Divine Teacher. With Me comes the light necessary for instant instruction on any given topic. You may say, "Give it to me all at once, God. If You are who You say, You can do that."

You are correct. I could do that, such is My power. But you, My friend, are not disposed to accept such an experience because My truth is all about love. Your little heart must be expanded first. We have to make room for all of this truth, which is filled with love. I want you to embark with Me on a journey. Walk with Me. Allow Me to draw you into your soul, into the mystical nature of your-self. Come to Me there so I can introduce you to the great truths about your family, the family of God. You will find such acceptance there. When you rest in My gaze in your soul, you will understand about love. You will, at the same time, understand about heaven, your ultimate home. I am calling to you now and I know that you hear Me. Come to Me. Stay with Me. Give Me the briefest chance to reveal Myself to you.

Jesus

As I draw you into the mystical nature of yourself, I draw you into My heart. My heart and your heart belong together. When you are with Me, you feel calm and accepted. You feel oneness with others because you experience community in your soul. If I am with each man as I am with you, then you are connected to each man through Me. Do you begin to understand the family of God? I love every man created. I have a good plan for every man created. This is My truth and, as you recall, I can never be where there is deceit. If I have a good agenda for every man created, and I have a good agenda for you, you are safe with Me and all mankind is safe with Me. If connected to Me, each person will serve his time on earth in mystical union with every other person and in mystical union with all of the saints in heaven. We are all connected. After this time of service, each man connected to Me comes home to Me and home to the family that loves him, awaits him, and welcomes him. There is no bad will on heaven's side. There is only acceptance and truth. I have such hope for you, My friend. All of your gifts originate in God and are an outgrowth of God's goodness. If you learn to understand Me, you will learn that I want to use your gifts to create harmony in your soul. When you use your gifts and energy for My purposes, you will benefit the whole world. It must be so because I have said it is so and I can speak only the truth. We are all connected. Would you like to benefit the world? Truly, you are capable of this and this is My plan for you. I have so much to give to you in terms of knowledge and wisdom. Teamed with Me, you will flourish and grow to heights you never dreamed possible. Rejoice. You are resting with God, the God of All. This God tells you today that you are loved and needed.

Jesus

Follow this path that springs up before you. Come to Me. Turn in My direction and I will reveal this path that I want you to take. You will feel lightness in your spirit, a relief. You will feel calm. Inside there will quietly burst forth a bud of hope. This bud will blossom, have no fear. The hope you feel in your soul is nourished by the time you spend with Me, seeking truth. I will see to it all. I need the smallest, even the most tremulous willingness.

You are hesitant to believe in Me. I know that. I understand everything that has gone before this moment in your life. Remember that I have all universal truth available to Me. In that respect, am I not a valuable person for you to know? Could you admit that I am possibly the most valuable person you could ever know? If you knew of someone on earth who had all truth about everything, who understood the purest facts and possessed the cleanest, most pristine vision of reality imaginable, would you not seek out this person's company? If you were wise, you would do so. If you were a man who desired truth, you would do so. If you were weary of lies and falseness, you would do so. My friend, if you seek truth, you must come with Me. If you seek acceptance, you must come to Me. If you want to be loved, you must rest in My heart because it is the only place where you will find the perfect security you crave. I am with you. I will never leave you. You could not escape My presence, even if you wanted to. You may as well get to know Me better so that you can decide whether you will reject Me or accept Me. This is the ultimate choice that will be yours. Just as you cannot escape My presence, you cannot escape this choice. It is yours. I want you to consider your options.

Jesus

My friend, this is between you and Me. By "this" I

refer to both this conversation and your ultimate decision of whether to accept Me or reject Me. When you are asked to make an important decision on earth, you consider your options. You take time and weigh both sides. Perhaps you waver between one course and another. I want you to consider both sides of this decision. If you accept Me, you will have entry into the most loving and secure family of all. If you accept Me, you will have security for the rest of your life in that I will lay out the course in front of you, guiding you, protecting you, and never leaving you. If you accept Me, you will come to heaven in triumph, bringing with you the great benefits that your cooperation secured for your family. You will walk in truth and in calm. Your life on earth will not suddenly become easy, but it will be filled with God's peace and God's grace.

If you reject Me, you will continue on, vulnerable to the deceit of My enemy. You will delude yourself at times, thinking that you are wise. Perhaps you will feel superior to many of your brothers and sisters, but I tell you today, in all of My truth, that the most humble one in heaven holds all of God's mysteries in his soul. You will not be privy to these mystical realities if you reject Me. How could you be if you did not want to be?

I conclude with one of the greatest truths of all and that is that I do not force My children to choose Me. I do not force humanity to work for heaven. If I did, we would not have a family, but a master and his slaves. No. This is not for Me and this is not for you. The heavenly Kingdom would not be the heavenly Kingdom if it were not filled with willing and beloved children. Everyone in heaven works for each other in great joy. Everyone in heaven works for our family members on earth in great hope. As you read these words, there is great hope in heaven that you will choose Me, Jesus Christ, and embark upon the journey to truth. It is here for you. I have truth and I have a course laid out for you that will bring you to this destination.

I love you. I will take care of you. Choose Me and I will begin to reveal Myself to you. You will know peace, My friend. You will know security. You will know joy for all eternity. This is your inheritance and I am your God. Allow nothing to divert you from the truth that I am Jesus Christ and I love you. I come today to announce Myself to you and to save you. Come. Trust Me. Be with Me. I will protect you.

Heaven Speaks to Those
Who Experience Tragedy

Jesus

December 12, 2006

Life on earth is filled with change. If you look back on any life, you can see marking points where that life changed. Sometimes change comes in a predictable and expected manner, as in the movement into a vocation for which a person prepared. Sometimes change comes in an abrupt manner, as in situations where a person is injured or dies unexpectedly. It is this, the change viewed as a tragedy, that I wish to discuss today. My friend, there are events in every life that stand out as difficult and life-altering. This tragedy, this abrupt change of course, will stand out to you, I know. When you feel a sense of shock, a sense of stunning upset in your life, you must look for Me. I am there. I do not remain with My children, day after day, and then abandon them when they most need My support. Your grief is understandable and I will support you in it. You will not always understand why I allowed a certain thing to happen. In your expected inability to understand, you will challenge Me. You will say, "God, how could You have allowed this? God, where are You? God, why have You abandoned us?"

My friends, bring those questions directly to Me because I, Myself, am the most sympathetic listener when it comes to these heartfelt cries of anguish. You see, I cried these cries Myself. In My humanity, on the cross, I felt abandoned. In My humanity, on the cross, I questioned the value of God's plan. From My viewpoint, nailed to a piece of wood and raised aloft as a subject of total rejection and derision, it appeared that I suffered more than anyone. It appeared that none could know the extent of My pain. My beloved child, I tell you this so that you will understand that I, your Savior, grasp the depth of your pain. I will walk you through each moment of anguish, surrounding you with heaven's graces. No. You will not be left to walk alone through this tragedy.

St. Ambrose

My friend, rest with heaven a moment. At this time, it is important to remember that every life on earth is finite. When a child is born into a family, there is no way to know the extent of his life. There is no way to know the plan for that life. There is no way to know the sufferings and joys that will provide formation for that life in order to bring that child to knowledge of God to the extent that God has intended. We, humanity, simply do not know God's plan. If we accept this truth, we will move through our lives with a greater appreciation for the possibility of change. As you walk the earth today, which one of you knows whether or not you will be walking the earth tomorrow? No person on earth today is assured that he will be on earth tomorrow. Clearly, it was the same in my lifetime. Nobody knows whether or not this is his last day to serve on earth. In the same way, perhaps you celebrate good health today. Does this mean you have a guarantee of good health tomorrow? Can you prevent a circumstance that will alter your health or your ability to serve tomorrow as you serve today? No, dear friend, you cannot. Accept this fact and you will serve in greater humility, aware that God could allow your course to be changed at any moment.

You, my beloved friend, are experiencing this today. You are stunned by the change in course that God has allowed for you or for someone you love. I understand. I want to compare your situation to that of Jesus Christ's situation in His Passion because we, as Christians, must compare every experience to the Lord's experience so we will understand how to best conduct ourselves. Jesus suffered terribly before He died. His death was not sudden in terms of time in that He carried a cross to an expected death. That stated, can anyone be prepared for a torture and death such as He experienced? What preparation can there be for a mother to bring her to peace about such torturous treatment of her only child? Can a mother ever reconcile herself to a child's death, particularly such a violent death? My friend, you are possibly shaking your head, saying, "No. It would be impossible for a mother to reconcile herself to the cruelty levied at her Son." I understand. I agree with you. Taken by itself, without the illumination of God, it would be impossible to accept such a set of circumstances. In the same way, if you take your tragedy by itself, without God's illumination, you may find it impossible to reconcile yourself to it.

Our mother, Mary, did reconcile her mother's heart to the will of the Father. She did this by joining herself to God's will in each moment. Mary never separated her life and every circumstance around her from trust in the Father's plan. This, most assuredly, does not mean that Mary was given extraordinary light to understand God's plan in each moment. On the contrary, Mary had to practice trust in a disciplined way because there were more moments of fog for her than clarity in terms of why God was allowing or advancing His plan in a given manner. Poor little mother, so worried for her Son's safety and happiness. Can we say that Mary proceeded wisely, despite her anguish? Yes, truly, we can say this. Mary proceeded wisely because she trusted that even though her Son suffered, even though her Son died, God's plan was the best plan, both for her Son and for humanity.

My friend, perhaps you cannot see God's plan illuminated in your grief and your pain. We understand. We will not leave you as you move through this period of shock. Believe me, one day you will see God's plan and you will look back to this day with perfect understanding, saying, "Yes, I understand God's plan."

St. Ambrose

Some of us walk through life trusting God. It is a habit that we have practiced for many years and it comes more or less naturally to us after a time. When a tragedy occurs in our life, we proceed through it in trust, despite our anguish, simply because this is what we have done in the past. Oh, my beloved friend, how priceless is the discipline of holiness. Perhaps you do not trust God and you do not have a habit to fall back on. Perhaps you are angry at God over something else and now you are confronted with this tragedy. You are possibly experiencing a grave temptation to hate God because you are blaming Him for this tragedy. I can see how this would happen. I can see how events in your life have brought you to this point. This is not a good place for you. You know that. You are angry at God and yet God is not angry at you. You want to cast God out of your life and yet God does not want to cast you out of His presence. God, on the contrary, wants to pull you up against Himself so that He can console you. God has so many things to whisper in your ear. You will not be able to accept this tragedy if you do not allow God to help you. "Fine," you say, rebelliously. "I do not and I will not accept this tragedy, ever." Hmm. My friend, the tragedy is not going away, simply because you pledge to reject it. The tragedy has occurred. You cannot control tragedy any more than you can control death. You will die and this pain will have ended. What then? Will you wait until that moment to reconcile with God and your heavenly family? You are a person of good will. Surely you will not choose eternal separation from God. That would not be good for you. Do you want to spend eternity with your loved ones? Perhaps you should consider that your loved ones wish to spend eternity with you. I can promise you this today. Your loved ones want you to be with them in heaven. They are telling me this now. They are here with me, watching you, surrounding you with prayer, and they are asking that you accept God's grace into your heart. You see, you are not alone. You are not abandoned. God allows all those who have gone before you to help you in times of difficulty. There are many here who seek your peace. Ask God to give you the grace to reconcile yourself to His will. He will do so. I will help you. Throw yourself into the arms of your beloved Savior and allow Him to protect you and comfort you.

St. Ambrose

My friend, my beloved family member, I am going to help you. Take these words into your heart. The graces attached to them will sustain you. You will see that very often the kindest, holiest people are those who have experienced tragedies. They understand that great pain comes into every life. Sometimes, there is nothing to comfort you, no drink of water in your parched thirst for yesterday. Do you wish to undo God's will? Would you like to be one who rejects God's will and marks out his own path to Christ? This would be like driving a car while blinded. Only God can see your destination and only God can see the best course for you to travel to arrive there. Perhaps there is great guilt in your grief. Perhaps you hold yourself accountable for something that you feel contributed to the tragedy before you. Oh dear friend, please, give this guilt to God. Allow God to take this away and let Him do with it as He wishes. If you turn to God now, He will remove this burden from you and put it exactly where it needs to be. God will burn it up in the flames of His passionate love for you. If you need to confess a sin, do so. Otherwise, consign your guilt to Jesus as something that He must take care of for you. The Lord, in His great mercy, rejoices in exactly this type of request. Do not revisit yesterday, except as it causes you joy. I want to say a final word to you. The only way to travel the road to heaven is in trust. If you trust God, even the littlest bit, you will make progress and you will stay on the path to Him. You will proceed in some measure of peace and you will remain calm. Dearest friend, when you feel that you cannot remain calm, call on heaven. You can tell heaven that you have an emergency. Heaven will respond at once, bringing graces of trust and calm to you. If you trust in heaven, and you should, you will understand that heaven never abandons anyone. Heaven does not abandon you any more than heaven abandons those around you who also suffer at this time. Ask for graces for those around you and they will receive graces because of your request. If you pray for others in a time of such great pain, heaven will flood others with graces because heaven views this prayer, made in sorrow, as the most beautiful act of trust. The angels delight in this prayer and bring this prayer before the Father as evidence of man's respect for His dominion. God the Father, in turn, unleashes a torrent of conversion, healing, and calming graces for all involved in the tragedy. Truly, the Father orders the angels and saints to benefit thousands from such a situation. Talk to heaven and you and all those around you will be blessed powerfully.

Blessed Mother

My poor little child, how you suffer. There are times when suffering is so great that a little one cannot even feel the comfort that is lavished upon him. It is this way for you now. In your grief, you stagger, but you are supported. I know that you do not always feel this support. We accept this. Later, when you come to heaven, you will marvel at the generosity of heaven as you understand the great lengths heaven went to in order to support you through this tragedy. Dear beloved child of the Father, rest in your little soul. You are like a wounded one who requires heavenly nursing. We will nurse you. I will watch closely and take each opportunity to send you examples of heaven's tender care for you. God has a plan and you are part of that plan just as I was part of God's plan. I am playing my part in God's plan now in speaking these words to you. Why do we use words? Little child, we use words to communicate truth because we are holy souls, filled with God's integrity. These words represent God's truth. If a person sends a letter, filled with love, can you say that the person sent words? Is it not more accurate to say that the person has sent love and kindness which brings also encouragement? On earth, in the lim-

ited view of those who do not yet experience heaven, perhaps it is true that a word is simply a word, representing a concept. In heaven, which is where we speak from, a word is much more. These words carry with them heavenly graces of truth, of comfort and of joy. My love for you, which is part of God's love for you, flows out from this page to your heart. My intercession for you is taking place as you read these words. Heaven is with you, I promise you. I am your mother and you are my beloved child. Turn your face to me and I will give you heavenly comfort that cannot be seen or understood. You will know that I am with you by the calming graces that come with me wherever I go. I am calm because I see God's plan. I will give you this calm and help you to see, at the very least, that God has a plan for you and that it includes this tragedy. I am with you, little dove. Your pain will not be without value and every tear you cry will be a tear that is noticed by heaven. Peace now, as we walk with you through this time of grief. We will give you the graces you need to cope today and to grow in holiness tomorrow. All is well. Heaven surrounds you.

Appendix

Guidelines for Lay Apostles

As lay apostles of Jesus Christ the Returning King, we agree to perform our basic obligations as practicing Catholics. Additionally, we will adopt the following spiritual practices, as best we can:

1. **Allegiance Prayer** and **Morning Offering**, plus a brief prayer for the Holy Father
2. **Eucharistic Adoration**, one hour per week
3. **Prayer Group Participation**, monthly, at which we pray the Luminous Mysteries of the Holy Rosary and read the Monthly Message
4. **Monthly Confession**
5. Further, we will follow the example of Jesus Christ as set out in the Holy Scripture, treating all others with His patience and kindness.

Allegiance Prayer

Dear God in Heaven, I pledge my allegiance to You. I give You my life, my work and my heart. In turn, give me the grace of obeying Your every direction to the fullest possible extent. Amen.

Morning Offering

O Jesus, through the Immaculate Heart of Mary, I offer You the prayers, works, joys and sufferings of this day, for all the intentions of Your Sacred Heart, in union with the Holy Sacrifice of the Mass throughout the world, in reparation for my sins, and for the intentions of the Holy Father. Amen.

Prayer for the Holy Father

Blessed Mother of Jesus, protect our Holy Father, Benedict XVI, and bless his intentions.

Five Luminous Mysteries

1. The Baptism of Jesus
2. The Wedding at Cana
3. The Proclamation of the Kingdom of God
4. The Transfiguration
5. The Institution of the Eucharist

Promise from Jesus to His Lay Apostles

May 12, 2005

Your message to souls remains constant. Welcome each soul to the rescue mission. You may assure each lay apostle that just as they concern themselves with My interests, I will concern Myself with theirs. They will be placed in My Sacred Heart and I will defend and protect them. I will also pursue complete conversion of each of their loved ones. So you see, the souls who serve in this rescue mission as My beloved lay apostles will know peace. The world cannot make this promise as only Heaven can bestow peace on a soul. This is truly Heaven's mission and I call every one of Heaven's children to assist Me. You will be well rewarded, My dear ones.

Prayers Taken from The Volumes

Prayers to God the Father

"I trust You, God. I offer You my pain in the spirit of acceptance and I will serve You in every circumstance."

"God my Father in Heaven, You are all mercy. You love me and see my every sin. God, I call on You now as the Merciful Father. Forgive my every sin. Wash away the stains on my soul so that I may once again rest in complete innocence. I trust You, Father in Heaven. I rely on You. I thank You. Amen."

"God my Father, calm my spirit and direct my path."

"God, I have made mistakes. I am sorry. I am Your child, though, and seek to be united to You."

"I believe in God. I believe Jesus is calling me. I believe my Blessed Mother has requested my help. Therefore I am going to pray on this day and every day."

"God my Father, help me to understand."

Prayers to Jesus

"Jesus, I give You my day."

"Jesus, how do You want to use me on this day? You have a willing servant in me, Jesus. Allow me to work for the Kingdom."

"Lord, what can I do today to prepare for Your coming? Direct me, Lord, and I will see to Your wishes."

"Lord, help me."

"Jesus, love me."

Prayers to the Angels

"Angels from Heaven, direct my path."

"Dearest angel guardian, I desire to serve Jesus by remaining at peace. Please obtain for me the graces necessary to maintain His divine peace in my heart."

Prayers for a Struggling Soul

"Jesus, what do You think of all this? Jesus, what do You want me to do for this soul? Jesus, show me how to bring You into this situation."

"Angel guardian, thank you for your constant vigil over this soul. Saints in Heaven, please assist this dear angel."

Prayers for Children

"God in Heaven, You are the Creator of all things. Please send Your graces down upon our world."

"Jesus, I love You."

"Jesus, I trust in You. Jesus, I trust in You. Jesus, I trust in You."

"Jesus, I offer You my day."

"Mother Mary, help me to be good."

How to Recite the Chaplet of Divine Mercy

The Chaplet of Mercy is recited using ordinary Rosary beads of five decades. The Chaplet is preceded by two opening prayers from the *Diary* of Saint Faustina and followed by a closing prayer.

1. Make the Sign of the Cross

In the name of the Father, and of the Son, and of the Holy Spirit. Amen.

2. Optional Opening Prayers

You expired, Jesus, but the source of life gushed forth for souls, and the ocean of mercy opened up for the whole world. O Fount of Life, unfathomable Divine Mercy, envelop the whole world and empty Yourself out upon us.

O Blood and Water, which gushed forth from the Heart of Jesus as a fountain of mercy for us, I trust in You!

3. Our Father

Our Father, who art in Heaven, hallowed be Thy name. Thy Kingdom come. Thy will be done on earth as it is in Heaven. Give us this day our daily bread. And forgive us our trespasses, as we forgive those who trespass against us. And lead us not into temptation, but deliver us from evil. Amen.

4. Hail Mary

Hail Mary, full of grace, the Lord is with thee. Blessed art thou among women, and blessed is the fruit of thy womb, Jesus. Holy Mary, Mother of God, pray for us sinners, now and at the hour of our death. Amen.

5. The Apostles' Creed

I believe in God, the Father Almighty, Creator of Heaven and earth. I believe in Jesus Christ, His only Son, Our Lord. He was conceived by the power of the Holy Spirit and born of the Virgin Mary. He suffered under Pontius Pilate, was crucified, died, and was buried. He descended to the dead. On the third day He rose again. He ascended into Heaven, and is seated at the right hand of the Father. He will come again to judge the living and the dead. I believe in the Holy Spirit, the holy Catholic Church, the Communion of Saints, the forgiveness of sins, the resurrection of the body, and life everlasting. Amen.

6. The Eternal Father

Eternal Father, I offer You the Body and Blood, Soul and Divinity of Your Dearly Beloved Son, our Lord, Jesus Christ, in atonement for our sins and those of the whole world.

7. On the Ten Small Beads of Each Decade

For the sake of His Sorrowful Passion, have mercy on us and on the whole world.

8. Repeat for the remaining decades

Saying the "Eternal Father" (6) on the "Our Father" bead and then 10 "For the sake of His Sorrowful Passion" (7) on the following "Hail Mary" beads.

9. Conclude with Holy God

Holy God, Holy Mighty One, Holy Immortal One, have mercy on us and on the whole world.

10. Optional Closing Prayer

Eternal God, in whom mercy is endless and the treasury of compassion—inexhaustible, look kindly upon us and increase Your mercy in us, that in difficult moments we might not despair nor become despondent, but with great confidence submit ourselves to Your holy will, which is Love and Mercy itself.

To learn more about the image of The Divine Mercy, the Chaplet of Divine Mercy and the series of revelations given to St. Faustina Kowalska please contact:

Marians of the Immaculate Conception
Stockbridge, Massachusetts 01263
Telephone 800-462-7426
www.marian.org

How to Pray the Rosary

1. Make the Sign of the Cross and say the "Apostles Creed."
2. Say the "Our Father."
3. Say three "Hail Marys."
4. Say the "Glory be to the Father."
5. Announce the First Mystery; then say the "Our Father."
6. Say ten "Hail Marys," while meditating on the Mystery.
7. Say the "Glory be to the Father." After each decade say the following prayer requested by the Blessed Virgin Mary at Fatima: "O my Jesus, forgive us our sins, save us from the fires of hell, lead all souls to Heaven, especially those in most need of Thy mercy."
8. Announce the Second Mystery: then say the "Our Father." Repeat 6 and 7 and continue with the Third, Fourth, and Fifth Mysteries in the same manner.
9. Say the "Hail, Holy Queen" on the medal after the five decades are completed.

As a general rule, depending on the season, the Joyful Mysteries are said on Monday and Saturday; the Sorrowful Mysteries on Tuesday and Friday; the Glorious Mysteries on Wednesday and Sunday; and the Luminous Mysteries on Thursday.

Papal Reflections of the Mysteries

The Joyful Mysteries

The Joyful Mysteries are marked by the joy radiating from the event of the Incarnation. This is clear from the very first mystery, the Annunciation, where Gabriel's greeting to the Virgin of Nazareth is linked to an invitation to messianic joy: "Rejoice, Mary." The whole of salvation... had led up to this greeting.

(Prayed on Mondays and Saturdays, and optional on Sundays during Advent and the Christmas Season.)

The Luminous Mysteries

Moving on from the infancy and the hidden life in Nazareth to the public life of Jesus, our contemplation brings us to those mysteries which may be called in a special way "mysteries of light." Certainly, the whole mystery of Christ is a mystery of light. He is the "Light of the world" (John 8:12). Yet this truth emerges in a special way during the years of His public life. (Prayed on Thursdays.)

The Sorrowful Mysteries

The Gospels give great prominence to the Sorrowful Mysteries of Christ. From the beginning, Christian piety, especially during the Lenten devotion of the Way of the Cross, has focused on the individual moments of the Passion, realizing that here is found the culmination of the revelation of God's love and the source of our salvation. (Prayed on Tuesdays and Fridays, and optional on Sundays during Lent.)

The Glorious Mysteries

"The contemplation of Christ's face cannot stop at the image of the Crucified One. He is the Risen One!" The Rosary has always expressed this knowledge born of faith and invited the believer to pass beyond the darkness of the Passion in order to gaze upon Christ's glory in the Resurrection and Ascension... Mary herself would be raised to that same glory in the Assumption. (Prayed on Wednesdays and Sundays.)

From the *Apostolic Letter The Rosary of the Virgin Mary*, Pope John Paul II, Oct. 16, 2002.

Prayers of the Rosary

The Sign of the Cross

In the name of the Father, and of the Son, and of the Holy Spirit. Amen.

The Apostles' Creed

I believe in God, the Father Almighty, Creator of Heaven and earth. I believe in Jesus Christ, His only Son, Our Lord. He was conceived by the power of the Holy Spirit and born of the Virgin Mary. He suffered under Pontius Pilate, was crucified, died, and was buried. He descended to the dead. On the third day He rose again. He ascended into Heaven, and is seated at the right hand of the Father. He will come again to judge the living and the dead. I believe in the Holy Spirit, the holy Catholic Church, the Communion of Saints, the forgiveness of sins, the resurrection of the body, and life everlasting. Amen.

Our Father

Our Father, who art in Heaven, hallowed be Thy name. Thy Kingdom come. Thy will be done on earth as it is in Heaven. Give us this day our daily bread. And forgive us our trespasses, as we forgive those who trespass against us. And lead us not into temptation, but deliver us from evil. Amen.

Hail Mary

Hail Mary, full of grace, the Lord is with thee. Blessed art thou among women, and blessed is the fruit of thy womb, Jesus. Holy Mary, Mother of God, pray for us sinners, now and at the hour of our death. Amen.

Glory Be to the Father

Glory be to the Father, and to the Son, and to the Holy Spirit. As it was in the beginning, is now, and ever shall be, world without end. Amen.

Hail Holy Queen

Hail, Holy Queen, Mother of Mercy, our life, our sweetness and our hope. To thee do we cry, poor banished children of Eve. To thee do we send up our sighs, mourning and weeping in this valley of tears. Turn then, most gracious Advocate, thine eyes of mercy towards us. And after this, our exile, show unto us the blessed fruit of thy womb, Jesus. O clement, O loving, O sweet Virgin Mary!

Pray for us, O Holy Mother of God.
That we may be made worthy of the promises of Christ.

The Mysteries

First Joyful Mystery:
The Annunciation

And when the angel had come to her, he said, "Hail, full of grace, the Lord is with thee. Blessed art thou among women."

(Luke 1:28)

One Our Father, Ten Hail Marys,
One Glory Be, etc.

Fruit of the Mystery: ***Humility***

Second Joyful Mystery:
The Visitation

Elizabeth was filled with the Holy Spirit and cried out in a loud voice: "Blest are you among women and blest is the fruit of your womb." (Luke 1:41-42)

One Our Father, Ten Hail Marys,
One Glory Be, etc.

Fruit of the Mystery: ***Love of Neighbor***

Third Joyful Mystery:
The Birth of Jesus

She gave birth to her first-born Son and wrapped Him in swaddling clothes and laid Him in a manger, because there was no room for them in the place where travelers lodged. (*Luke* 2:7)

One *Our Father*, Ten *Hail Marys*,
One *Glory Be*, etc.

Fruit of the Mystery: ***Poverty***

Fourth Joyful Mystery:
The Presentation

When the day came to purify them according to the law of Moses, the couple brought Him up to Jerusalem so that He could be presented to the Lord, for it is written in the law of the Lord, "Every first-born male shall be consecrated to the Lord."

(*Luke* 2:22-23)

One *Our Father*, Ten *Hail Marys*,
One *Glory Be*, etc.

Fruit of the Mystery: ***Obedience***

Fifth Joyful Mystery:
The Finding of the Child Jesus in the Temple

On the third day they came upon Him in the temple sitting in the midst of the teachers, listening to them and asking them questions. (*Luke* 2:46)

One *Our Father*, Ten *Hail Marys*,
One *Glory Be*, etc.

Fruit of the Mystery: ***Joy in Finding Jesus***

First Luminous Mystery:
The Baptism of Jesus

And when Jesus was baptized... the heavens were opened and He saw the Spirit of God descending like a dove, and alighting on Him, and lo, a voice from Heaven, saying "this is My beloved Son," with whom I am well pleased." (*Matthew* 3:16-17)

One *Our Father*, Ten *Hail Marys*,
One *Glory Be*, etc.

Fruit of the Mystery: ***Openness to the Holy Spirit***

Second Luminous Mystery:
The Wedding at Cana

His mother said to the servants, "Do whatever He tells you." . . .
Jesus said to them, "Fill the jars with water." And they filled them
up to the brim.

(John 2:5-7)

One Our Father, Ten Hail Marys,
One Glory Be, etc.

Fruit of the Mystery: ***To Jesus through Mary***

Third Luminous Mystery:
The Proclamation of the Kingdom of God

"And preach as you go, saying, 'The Kingdom of Heaven is at
hand.' Heal the sick, raise the dead, cleanse lepers, cast out
demons. You received without pay, give without pay."

(Matthew 10:7-8)

One Our Father, Ten Hail Marys,
One Glory Be, etc.

Fruit of the Mystery: ***Repentance and Trust in God***

Fourth Luminous Mystery:
The Transfiguration

And as He was praying, the appearance of His countenance was
altered and His raiment become dazzling white. And a voice came
out of the cloud saying, "This is My Son, My chosen; listen to Him!

(Luke 9:29, 35)

One Our Father, Ten Hail Marys,
One Glory Be, etc.

Fruit of the Mystery: ***Desire for Holiness***

Fifth Luminous Mystery:
The Institution of the Eucharist

And He took bread, and when He had given thanks He broke it and gave it to them, saying, "This is My body which is given for you." . . . And likewise the cup after supper, saying, "This cup which is poured out for you is the new covenant in My blood."
(Luke 22:19-20)

One Our Father, Ten Hail Marys,
One Glory Be, etc.

Fruit of the Mystery: ***Adoration***

First Sorrowful Mystery:
The Agony in the Garden

In His anguish He prayed with all the greater intensity, and His sweat became like drops of blood falling to the ground. Then He rose from prayer and came to His disciples, only to find them asleep, exhausted with grief.   (Luke 22:44-45)

One Our Father, Ten Hail Marys,
One Glory Be, etc.

Fruit of the Mystery: ***Sorrow for Sin***

Second Sorrowful Mystery:
The Scourging at the Pillar

Pilate's next move was to take Jesus and have Him scourged.
(John 19:1)

One Our Father, Ten Hail Marys,
One Glory Be, etc.

Fruit of the Mystery: ***Purity***

Third Sorrowful Mystery:
The Crowning with Thorns

They stripped off His clothes and wrapped Him in a scarlet military cloak. Weaving a crown out of thorns they fixed it on His head, and stuck a reed in His right hand...   (Matthew 27:28-29)

One Our Father, Ten Hail Marys,
One Glory Be, etc.

Fruit of the Mystery: ***Courage***

Fourth Sorrowful Mystery:
The Carrying of the Cross

... carrying the cross by Himself, He went out to what is called the Place of the Skull (in Hebrew, Golgotha).   (*John* 19:17)
One *Our Father*, Ten *Hail Marys*,
One *Glory Be*, etc.
Fruit of the Mystery: ***Patience***

Fifth Sorrowful Mystery:
The Crucifixion

Jesus uttered a loud cry and said, "Father, into Your hands I commend My spirit." After He said this, He expired. (*Luke* 23:46)
One *Our Father*, Ten *Hail Marys*,
One *Glory Be*, etc.
Fruit of the Mystery: ***Perseverance***

First Glorious Mystery:
The Resurrection

You need not be amazed! You are looking for Jesus of Nazareth, the one who was crucified. He has been raised up; He is not here. See the place where they laid Him."   (*Mark* 16:6)
One *Our Father*, Ten *Hail Marys*,
One *Glory Be*, etc.
Fruit of the Mystery: ***Faith***

Second Glorious Mystery:
The Ascension

Then, after speaking to them, the Lord Jesus was taken up into Heaven and took His seat at God's right hand.   (*Mark* 16:19)
One *Our Father*, Ten *Hail Marys*,
One *Glory Be*, etc.
Fruit of the Mystery: ***Hope***

Third Glorious Mystery:
The Descent of the Holy Spirit

All were filled with the Holy Spirit. They began to express themselves in foreign tongues and make bold proclamation as the Spirit prompted them. *(Acts* 2:4)

One *Our Father*, Ten *Hail Marys*,
One *Glory Be*, etc.

Fruit of the Mystery: ***Love of God***

Fourth Glorious Mystery:
The Assumption

You are the glory of Jerusalem... you are the splendid boast of our people... God is pleased with what you have wrought. May you be blessed by the Lord Almighty forever and ever.

(Judith 15:9-10)

One *Our Father*, Ten *Hail Marys*,
One *Glory Be*, etc.

Fruit of the Mystery: ***Grace of a Happy Death***

Fifth Glorious Mystery:
The Coronation

A great sign appeared in the sky, a woman clothed with the sun, with the moon under her feet, and on her head a crown of twelve stars. *(Revelation* 12:1)

One *Our Father*, Ten *Hail Marys*,
One *Glory Be*, etc.

Fruit of the Mystery: ***Trust in Mary's Intercession***

The Volumes

Direction for Our Times
as given to Anne, a lay apostle

Volume One: *Thoughts on Spirituality*
Volume Two: *Conversations with the Eucharistic Heart of Jesus*
Volume Three: *God the Father Speaks to His Children*
The Blessed Mother Speaks to Her Bishops and Priests
Volume Four: *Jesus the King*
Heaven Speaks to Priests
Jesus Speaks to Sinners
Volume Six: *Heaven Speaks to Families*
Volume Seven: *Greetings from Heaven*
Volume Nine: *Angels*
Volume Ten: *Jesus Speaks to His Apostles*

Volumes 5 and 8 will be printed at a later date.

The Volumes are now available in PDF format
for free download and printing from our website:
www.directionforourtimes.org.
We encourage everyone to print and distribute them.

The Volumes are also available at your local bookstore.

The "Heaven Speaks" Booklets
Direction for Our Times
as given to Anne, a lay apostle

The following booklets are available individually from Direction for Our Times:

Heaven Speaks About Abortion
Heaven Speaks About Addictions
Heaven Speaks to Victims of Clerical Abuse
Heaven Speaks to Consecrated Souls
Heaven Speaks About Depression
Heaven Speaks About Divorce
Heaven Speaks to Prisoners
Heaven Speaks to Soldiers
Heaven Speaks About Stress
Heaven Speaks to Young Adults

Heaven Speaks to Those Away from the Church
Heaven Speaks to Those Considering Suicide
Heaven Speaks to Those Who Do Not Know Jesus
Heaven Speaks to Those Who Are Dying
Heaven Speaks to Those Who Experience Tragedy
Heaven Speaks to Those Who Fear Purgatory
Heaven Speaks to Those Who Have Rejected God
Heaven Speaks to Those Who Struggle to Forgive
Heaven Speaks to Those Who Suffer from Financial Need
Heaven Speaks to Parents Who Worry About
   Their Children's Salvation

All twenty of the "Heaven Speaks" booklets are now available for free download and printing from our website www.directionforourtimes.org. We encourage everyone to print and distribute these booklets.

Other Written Works by Anne, a lay apostle

Climbing the Mountain

This book contains the fascinating story of how the rescue mission began and how it has blossomed into a worldwide apostolate under the watchful eye and in complete obedience to the Church. It is the story of The Lay Apostolate of Jesus Christ the Returning King.

Also featured is a summary of Anne's mystical experiences of Heaven. She describes the heavenly home that has been created for God's children. Reading these accounts, you will learn that in Heaven we will experience constant unity with Jesus. Anne also confirms that souls in Heaven work together to assist in answering the prayers of God's earthly children. At one point in time Jesus tells Anne, *"...you are a child of God and you have every right to be here."*

In the section entitled "Climbing the Mountain," Anne writes about her vision of the personal call to holiness that we all must hear.

It concludes with a reprint of the first ten "Heaven Speaks" booklets: Abortion, Addictions, Victims of Clerical Abuse, Consecrated Souls, Depression, Divorce, Prisoners, Soldiers, Stress, and Young Adults.

This is a book to be treasured as it reveals the intimate love of the Savior for each soul. Every reader will be called to great rejoicing, for truly, God's Kingdom comes.

The Mist of Mercy

Anne begins this book by telling us that the enemy of God is present on earth and a battle is being waged for souls. Satan is trying to destroy God's plan for us, which is unity with Him in Heaven for eternity. We must be alert to these efforts and be armed for the battle. This is the reality of spiritual warfare.

Following is a section entitled *Snapshots of Reality* which is a collection of short stories depicting realistic earthly struggles while including a glimpse of these same situations from the heavenly perspective and how our friends, the saints, act on our behalf more than we can imagine.

Also in this book is Anne's account of her mystical experiences of Purgatory. She tells us of the souls she saw there and describes the prayers they prayed and the remorse they felt for the choices they had made on earth which were against the will of God. You will be happy to learn that Purgatory is a great mercy of God and allows each soul there the perfect experience of preparation for eternity in Heaven.

The last section is a reprint of the Monthly Messages from Jesus Christ dated from December 1, 2004 through June 1, 2006.

Serving in Clarity

This book could be described as the guidebook for lay apostles who wish to serve Jesus Christ the Returning King. In essence, it is the walking guide, given to us by Heaven, describing how to obtain clarity so that our path up the Mountain of Holiness can be clearly identified.

The writing includes locutions from Jesus and Mary, encouraging us to trust that Heaven is sending extraordinary graces so that we will say "yes" to helping Jesus usher in the Age of Obedience.

Anne then shares her insight on how we should live our lives in love, holiness and obedience to the Church. Also included are vignettes of real life challenges that priests and people faced while serving in their vocations.

Especially compelling is the description of Anne's mystical experiences of the Mountain of Holiness, where Jesus showed her the current condition of the world so that lay apostles would be encouraged to participate in God's rescue mission for souls.

Reprinted in this book is *In Defense of Obedience and Reflections on the Priesthood*, as well as the Monthly Messages from Jesus dated July 26 through June 2008.

Serving in Clarity is a gift for all those who are serious about learning God's will for their life.

In Defense of Obedience
and
Reflections on the Priesthood

This work by Anne consists of two essays on topics close to the heart of Jesus. The first is entitled *In Defense of Obedience* and the second is entitled *Reflections on the Priesthood*.

In Defense of Obedience is a serious call to return to a spirit of obedience to the Magisterium of the Church. Obedience to the Church is a must for every apostle, laity and clergy alike.

Anne's essay on the priesthood gives us the smallest glimpse of the love our Lord has for the men who hear and answer His call. We read the depth of the connection Jesus has with these men and how they are united in a most unique way to the Sacred Heart of Jesus and the Immaculate Heart of Mary. This is also a gentle reminder that we are called to love and support our priests who serve us in their humanity but with a heavenly dignity bestowed upon them from heaven by Jesus Christ, the First Priest.

Interviews with Anne, a lay apostle

VHS tapes and DVDs featuring Anne, a lay apostle have been produced by Focus Worldwide Network and can be purchased by visiting our website at:

www.directionforourtimes.org

This book is part of a non-profit mission.
Our Lord has requested that we
spread these words internationally.

Please help us.

If you would like to assist us financially,
please send your tax-deductible contribution
to the address below:

Direction for Our Times
9000 West 81st Street
Justice, Illinois 60458

www.directionforourtimes.org

Email: contactus@directionforourtimes.com
Phone: 708-496-9300

Direction for Our Times Ireland
Drumacarrow
Bailieborough
County Cavan.
Republic of Ireland

www.directionforourtimes.org

Email: contactus@dfot.ie
Phone: 353-(0)42-969-4947 or 353-(0)42-969-4734

Direction for Our Times is a 501(c)(3)
not-for-profit corporation. Contributions are
deductible to the extent provided by law.

Jesus gives Anne a message for the world on
the first of each month. To receive the
monthly messages you may access our
website at www.directionforourtimes.org
or call us at 708-496-9300
to be placed on our mailing list.